LITTLE BOOK OF THE
RUGBY
WORLD CUP

THE GREATEST SHOW ON EARTH

LITTLE BOOK OF THE
RUGBY WORLD CUP

This edition first published in the UK in 2007
By Green Umbrella

© Green Umbrella Publishing 2007

www.greenumbrella.co.uk

Publishers Jules Gammond & Vanessa Gardner

Printed and bound in China

ISBN-13: 978-1-905828-37-1

Contents

Chapter 1

The World Cup
Humble beginnings

ALTHOUGH THE FIRST RUGBY World Cup was held in 1987, ever since the first Test matches, in 1871, sides across the world have claimed the unofficial title of the best rugby team on the planet.

At the start only England and Scotland battled for the title but by the 1920s it was accepted that the epic series between New Zealand and South Africa was deciding who were the unofficial world champions.

Other sides – most notably Wales in the early 1970s – laid claim to their unofficial title but for the decades either side of the war it was either the Springboks or the All Blacks who were the team to beat.

BELOW An early match between England and Scotland in the Athletic Grounds at Richmond, 1891

The closest rugby got to anointing an official world champion before 1987 was at the Olympic Games, where rugby was included in four Games between 1900 and 1928.

France won the first gold medal and USA the last before the Olympic committee removed rugby from their list of sports.

With football starting its World Cup in Uruguay in 1930, it was inevitable that rugby would go the same way at some point. Perhaps the only mystery is why it took so long?

The length of the time could probably be attributed to rugby's roots as an amateur sport.

Some leading nations were fervent campaigners of the amateur traditions right up until the game turned professional, in 1995. Some, like England, even opposed the World Cup when it was first mooted in the late 1970s, for fear of it leading to a professional game.

It was not until late 1983 that the Australian Rugby Union and New Zealand Rugby Football Union submitted written proposals to the International Rugby Board (IRB) for a World Cup.

Neither was aware of the other's proposal with Australia wanting to stage a tournament to coincide with their Bicentenary in 1988 and New Zealand proposing the previous year.

Both proposals were turned down but the two countries pooled their resources to conduct a feasibility study to be presented at the IRB's annual meeting in March 1985.

But it took the IRB until 1985 before they took their momentous decision, at their annual meeting in Paris, two years after the similar proposal was rejected.

New Zealand had been at the centre of the campaign for a World Cup since 1983, Australia joining the campaign a year later.

At the 1985 meeting - chaired by Australia's Dr Roger Vanderfield - it certainly wasn't a unanimous decision with the British and Irish unions initially sceptical, although today the Rugby

World Cup is one of the top three sporting events (behind the Olympics and the Football World Cup) in the world.

Only a two-thirds majority was in fact required at the IRB Executive and it was resolved to stage a 16-team tournament.

France were in favour of the proposal on one condition: that the Tournament would not be restricted to the eight IRB members but would involve other countries to enable the game to reach a broader audience.

No one at that 1985 meeting could have considered how quickly the Rugby World Cup would grow, and the multi-million pound event staged by Australia in 2003 – that captivated

ABOVE During the 1924 Olympics, rugby was played at the Colombes Stadium in Paris

ABOVE Francois Pienaar holds the World Cup aloft and salutes the crowd after South Africa's win – following extra time – in 1995

the tradition in the 1980s – the IRB announced the new tournament, after the New Zealand and Australia rugby unions presented their feasibility study. The IRB said: "This study was presented to the board and has been considered in detail by each member union. Following very full discussion, the board has agreed to proceed with the staging of a competition in 1987." Hardly the fanfare that you would expect today, but it still signalled the beginning of a tournament that has grown hugely each time. Those board members couldn't have imagined how it would have developed over the following 20 years.

They settled on 1987 as the year, for the first one, thereby avoiding any clash with the Olympic Games, FIFA World Cup or European Football Championship. This decision has been one of the key reasons for its success.

The first tournament was staged in May and June 1987, but by the time the 2011 tournament was set – for New Zealand – the IRB resolved to make the desired window September and October.

This decision over the months in which it is staged has met with dismay in the British and Irish unions as it

countries across the world – was a stunning success.

So nervous was the IRB about the World Cup, initially there were no plans for a second World Cup, but today we couldn't imagine the rugby world without it.

In a rather understated way – as was

means they cannot stage their lucrative November internationals every four years, having a big effect on their financial planning.

Back in 1987, the board set up a committee to control all aspects of the World Cup and appointed Australia and New Zealand to carry out the organisation and planning.

The five-man committee, chaired by England's former British and Irish Lion, John Kendall-Carpenter, also included Australia's Ross Turnbull, Keith Rowlands of Wales and Irishman Ronnie Dawson.

One person who played a key role in this journey was the late Vernon Pugh QC, the IRB and Rugby World Cup Ltd chairman. Pugh's energy and vision was instrumental in expanding the governing body to include 94 full members and in building the profile of the sport's showpiece event.

The 16 teams to participate in 1987 were invited by the IRB, in great contrast to the almost three-year qualification tournament that took place to decide the 20 teams that took part in 2003.

"I vividly remember watching the inaugural World Cup as a gangly 16-year-old

experiencing the first stirrings of its potential; secretly desiring but never truly believing that one day I may have the chance to participate," explained John Eales, who won the World Cup twice, in 1991 and 1999, in Gerald Davies' History of the World Cup.

"For me the World Cup cannot be defined by a single movement but by the

LEFT John Eales holds the Webb Ellis trophy after the 1999 final between France and Australia which Australia won 35-12

camaraderie, the passion and the excitement that the tournament encapsulates. There was something personally special about each of the tournaments in which I was involved."

Back in 1987 South Africa missed out, due to the political situation in the country. At the time New Zealand and Australia – where the first World Cup would be held – had a ban on the granting of visas to South African sports people. This didn't stop South Africa voting in favour of the tournament but the ban – due to the presence of apartheid in South Africa – meant they also missed the 1991 World Cup, making their debut – with victory – in 1995.

Ireland turned out to be one of the main opponents to the World Cup, fearing that it would signal the end to tours by the British and Irish Lions. They were one of the last nations to finally accept their invitation to take part.

BELOW The crowd cheers the South African Springbok team during a victory parade through Johannesburg, 1995

And to address some of those concerns the IRB went to great lengths to stress the amateur ethos of the first World Cup.

"The thing that interests us is the need to shore up rather than undermine the amateur ethos of the game. We probed this side very carefully and we have established a number of procedures so that the tournament remains very much on an amateur basis," said John Kendall-Carpenter, chairman of the IRB governing committee.

The Lions, of course, prospered in the professional, World Cup era, deciding to stage their tours two years before the World Cup, in each four-year cycle. So the Lions toured in 1997, 2001 and 2005, to fit in around the World Cup.

The IRB oversaw the establishment of a company, Rugby World Cup Ltd, to run the tournament, a system that still exists today.

"Of all the many matters discussed by the Board," Kendall-Carpenter, the Somerset headmaster added, "the new competition has to be a major part of rugby's future. The Board must control the tournament in all aspects. It is essential that we get everything right." How prophetic those words were.

ABOVE Eden Park in 2006. By the time of the 2011 World Cup, there will be new stands, all with covered seats, and a significantly lower roof

After 2007, the World Cup will return to New Zealand in 2011, after they won a controversial vote from Japan and South Africa. When it arrives it will present a massive economic boost for the country.

New Zealand expects the 2011 World Cup to generate more than A$1.15 billion in total economic activity, and pump more than half a billion dollars into the New Zealand economy.

Auckland, as host of the World Cup Final, stands to gain around $240 million in additional gross domestic product. As games will be hosted around the country the economic benefits will be widespread.

Based on Australia's experience of hosting the 2003 Rugby World Cup, New Zealand can expect to attract as many as 66,000 international supporters, 2,500 international media and up to 2,500 corporate and VIP guests throughout the tournament, with many people going on to explore other parts of the country.

"Winning the right to host 2011 is an enormous honour and privilege but also an enormous responsibility," said NZ rugby spokesman Jock Hobbs.

1987
The big kick off

IT WASN'T EXACTLY JUMPERS FOR goalposts, more like Rugby in the Raw when the World Cup finally kicked off in 1987… light years away from the 2007 event.

The game may have been amateur but the rugby was far from it, bringing some unforgettable matches and performances from some of the world's greatest players.

It was also a great success off the field with 600,000 fans coming through the turnstiles, at an average of 18,750 per match.

This prompted the chairman of the organising committee John Kendall-Carpenter to announce: "As far as I am concerned, the future is assured. We will have an unstoppable base for a tournament in 1991." At the time no-one had committed to a second World Cup.

"Rugby is not a world game at the moment," he added. "It's strong in certain parts of the world and other countries are being brought up to that standard."

Australia – the joint host with New Zealand – had just completed a Grand Slam in Europe and went into the tournament as one of the favourites.

RIGHT Wales went on to finish third in 1987 after beating England

But the 1987 World Cup was all about their joint hosts, New Zealand, as the All Blacks left an indelible mark on the Rugby World Cup.

The 16 World Cup finalists were made up of the seven IRB full board members – England, Scotland, Ireland, Wales, France, Australia, New Zealand – and nine invited sides. The only side excluded was South Africa, still exiled from many sports due to their apartheid political system.

With the World Cup only devised two years before, there simply wasn't time for the worldwide qualification tournament we see today.

Invitations were sent to: Argentina, Fiji, Italy, Canada, Romania, Tonga, Japan, Zimbabwe and the United States as the Board tried to bring member unions from all parts of the world.

But as the matches proved, those nine invited sides were unable to keep pace with the stronger top seven, producing a pretty lopsided pool stage, Japan, Tonga and Zimbabwe failing to win a match between them, and the real rugby only starting in the quarter-finals.

The seven top nations were joined by Fiji in those quarter-finals, the Fijians going down 31-16, at Eden Park, to France, who made it into the semi-finals along with Wales, Australia and New Zealand.

With New Zealand scoring 190 points in their three pool games and thrashing Scotland 30-3 in the quarters, Wales were their unfortunate opponents in the semis. The All Blacks cruised into the final with a 49-6 victory, Wales' Huw Richards becoming the first man to be sent off in a World Cup match.

New Zealand just failed to average 50 points a match at the first World Cup, summing up how they dominated.

England's tournament ended in the last eight when they lost 16-3 to Wales

BELOW France on their way to beating Australia in the semi-final of the 1987 tournament

and were described as "dreadful" by the Daily Telegraph's rugby correspondent, John Mason.

"They were shorn of ideas, tactical appreciation and all three Wales tries came from English mistakes."

In the semi-final – between France and Australia – the crowd were privileged to see one of rugby's great tries in the history of the game, Serge Blanco finishing off a length of the field move to take his side through 30-24.

Australia held the lead three times in a pulsating match, before Blanco struck for the final time.

The French – who came into the game after winning a Five Nations Grand Slam – were sublime and in the Sunday Telegraph John Reason said; "I never thought I would live to see a game to rival the one between the Barbarians and New Zealand in 1973, but this one did. So much was happening in so many places, for so much of the time that this game will be remembered as long as the World Cup is played."

The only result verging on a shock came in the third-place play-off with Wales triumphing 22-21 over Australia.

In the final, France failed to find their semi-final form, New Zealand storming to the title with a 29-9 victory.

The first final – in front of a capacity 46,000 crowd at Eden Park – wasn't a classic but they rarely are with All

BELOW New Zealand get ready for their semi-final against Wales by performing their haka

Blacks kicker Grant Fox – who scored 126 points at the tournament – running the game, and slotting six successful kicks at goal. Captain David Kirk also scored a try, along with Michael Jones and John Kirwan. The All Blacks dominated from start to finish to become the first side to lift the Webb Ellis Cup.

There was scant consolation for France in the latter of the final stages when Pierre Berbizier ran in the only French try.

New Zealand were also lucky to have the man of the tournament, openside flanker Michael Jones, marauding through the tournament, with a series of memorable displays.

New Zealand's domination of the first World Cup came after they lost captain Andy Dalton in the run-up to the tournament, a certain Sean Fitzpatrick taking his place in the team and Kirk, as skipper.

"We had lost a Test to France the year before and they had won the last two Five Nations. What evolved in the game was not our prettiest rugby but it was our best. France asked a lot of us," said Kirk.

"Having seen France play Australia in that epic semi-final, we felt they had

left something on the field.

"The game sped by and the French were pretty physical. But once I scored I had a gut feeling and knew we'd be champions.

"When the whistle went, there was no massive relief moment as we knew we were going to win. I just remember making a dash off the field – in the days when spectators could still run on.

"Lifting the trophy was neither a real buzz nor an anti-climax. There was a touch of melancholy. It must be how people feel at the top of Everest. They only have 20 minutes there and won't ever be back. The only way back is down.

"But that melancholy was overwhelmed by joy. It was all pretty amazing."

1987 WORLD CUP STAT ATTACK

GROUP A

Australia	19	England	6
USA	21	Japan	18
England	60	Japan	7
Australia	47	USA	12
England	34	USA	6
Australia	42	Japan	23

Australia and England qualify

GROUP B

Canada	37	Tonga	4
Wales	13	Ireland	6
Wales	29	Tonga	16
Ireland	46	Canada	19
Wales	40	Canada	9
Ireland	32	Tonga	9

Wales and Ireland qualify

GROUP C

New Zealand	70	Italy	6
Fiji	28	Argentina	9
New Zealand	74	Fiji	13
Argentina	25	Italy	16
Italy	18	Fiji	15
New Zealand	46	Argentina	15

New Zealand and Fiji qualify

GROUP D

France	20	Scotland	20
Romania	21	Zimbabwe	20
France	55	Romania	12
Scotland	60	Zimbabwe	21
Scotland	55	Romania	28
France	70	Zimbabwe	12

France and Scotland qualify

QUARTER-FINALS

New Zealand	30	Scotland	3
Wales	16	England	3
France	31	Fiji	16
Australia	33	Ireland	15

THIRD PLACE PLAY-OFF

Wales	22	Australia	21

SEMI-FINALS

New Zealand	49	Wales	6
France	30	Australia	24

WORLD CUP FINAL

New Zealand	29	France	9

LEADING TRY SCORERS

C Green (NZ)	6
J Kirwan (NZ)	6
M Harrison (Eng)	5
J Gallagher (NZ)	5
A Whetton (NZ)	5
D Kirk (NZ)	5

LEADING POINTS SCORERS

G Fox (NZ)	126
M Lynagh (Aus)	69
G Hastings (Scot)	50
J Webb (Eng)	43
D Camberabero (Fr)	37
S Koroduadua (Fiji)	35

1991
Second time around

AFTER THE FIRST RUGBY WORLD Cup was held – in 1987 – in the southern hemisphere, it was clear the second event would move to the north and where better than in the Five Nations countries of England, Wales, Scotland, Ireland and France.

So much had changed in the rugby world since 1987, as the game raced towards professionalism, and significantly on the pitch England had emerged – once more – as a real force in the game.

England merely made up the numbers in 1987 but with a new coach – Geoff Cooke – and a new captain in Will Carling they had won a Five Nations Grand Slam in 1991, arriving at the tournament as one of the favourites.

They had the added incentive of the fact that the final this time would be played at their home ground of Twickenham.

Commercialism also arrived at the World Cup in a far bigger form than four years earlier. Television coverage had amounted to 28 hours in 1987 but four years later it was more than 100 hours, sponsors and suppliers providing support to the tune of £10 million, allowing the gross income to rise to just short of £40 million.

That income was turned into a profit

RIGHT New Zealand, here against Canada, with John Kirwan battling for the ball, failed to retain their title, losing in the semi-final

of almost £25 million, up considerably from the £120,000 made in 1987.

Many things might have changed but one thing that hadn't was the form of New Zealand's Michael Jones, who after scoring a try in the first game of the 1987 competition – against Italy – repeated the trick in 1991 as the World Cup opened with England v New Zealand at Twickenham.

The 18-12 win by New Zealand meant that England would have to take a hard road to the final. As others enjoyed the green pastures of Twickenham, England were forced to overcome France in Paris and Scotland in Edinburgh to take their place alongside Australia for the second World Cup final.

Many people chose to blame England's decision to move from a forward-dominated game plan to one which tried to master the arts of expansive rugby. But the fact that they fell at the final hurdle was due more to the Herculean efforts they had to summon in the matches before, just to make the final.

In the end their change of tactics didn't bring a solitary try, prop Tony Daly scrambling the only one of the game in the first half, following a lineout.

David Campese didn't score but it was always hard to keep the great Aussie wing out of the game. When he batted down a pass meant for the overlapping Rory Underwood, Twickenham held its breath, only to see referee Derek Bevan give a penalty, rather than the penalty try all of England craved.

"I'm happy England chanced their arm that day but I can't believe that people still go on about that one, insisting that Campo cost Underwood the score," said Australia captain Nick Farr-Jones.

"I don't know why as there's no way

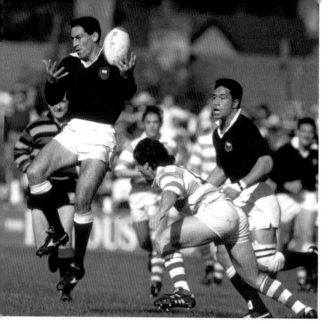

ABOVE Frank Bunce (left) of Western Samoa leaps for the ball during the match against Argentina, 1991

Queen and thought of my childhood memories of FA Cup captains walking up at Wembley.

"I knew that '91 was the final throw of the dice for me, which meant a lot of pressure and a lot of build-up and speculation."

If England faced the knockout rounds on the road then Australia could claim to an even harder route to the final, first having to win in Dublin against Ireland and then needing to beat holders New Zealand, in the same city.

The Ireland game was breathtaking with the 19-18 victory being handed to the Wallabies by a last-minute try from Michael Lynagh that broke the Irish hearts. Ireland thought they had won the quarter-final minutes before with a Gordon Hamilton try.

And the semi belonged to a certain David Campese, who often used the biggest stage as his chance to shine. One sensational try against the All Blacks – and creating another for Tim Horan – Campese saw them home 16-6. "That match was magnificent from start to finish," said Farr-Jones. "In fact, the first 40 minutes was the best rugby I'd ever been involved in.

"Campo defied all the logic of the

Underwood would have scored. He still had miles to cover and the defence would have come across."

England's only points came from the boot of Jonathan Webb, and Australia were home, Farr-Jones receiving the Webb Ellis Cup from Her Majesty the Queen.

"My main emotion was probably one of relief," Nick Farr-Jones added.

"For me, the biggest night next to Christmas was the FA Cup. I used to wake up to watch that and I remember walking up to get the trophy from the

game by running across the field before sealing a superb try. And that flip over the shoulder to Tim Horan for the second try was the stuff of legend."

In contrast to England, their neighbours Wales were close to shambolic when they arrived at the World Cup, after having lost 63-6 on a tour to Australia.

And it wasn't long before Wales were presenting the rugby world with the tournament's first real shock. Wales' defeat to Western Samoa, at Cardiff.

Little of course did the Welsh know at the time but players in the Samoa team that day, including Frank Bunce, Pat Lam and Brian Lima would go on to become world stars in their own right.

Samoa had arrived at the finals as part of the first qualification tournament. The sides were invited to participate in 1987 but in 1991 eight of the 16 places were filled by the quarter-finalists from four years earlier. Thirty-two countries fought out a qualification process for the remaining eight places.

Under New Zealand coach Bryan Williams, the Samoans turned the formbook upside down beating Wales 16-13 at Cardiff Arms Park. Wales may have been pool stage casualties but Scotland – with a Grand Slam of their own in 1990 – were a powerful force in 1991, enjoying their best World Cup campaign to date.

Scotland scored 122 points in their three pool matches and after accounting for Western Samoa – 28-6 – in the quarters they faced England at Murrayfield, in an epic encounter. Gavin Hastings –

BELOW David Campese scores for eventual winners, Australia, in the quarter-final against Ireland

so often the Scotland hero – missed a straightforward penalty with the scores at 6-6, leaving Rob Andrew the chance to send England into the final.

Scotland coach Ian McGeechan was in no doubt about the key to England's win.

"England wanted to strangle the game, we wanted to keep it alive," he said.

But England manager Geoff Cooke retorted: "We would love to have cut the Scots to pieces with scintillating back play but it's not quite as easy as that."

If Scotland were unfortunate to suffer from the boot of Andrew then Ireland must still be wondering how they failed to make the semi-finals, after that heart-stopping match against eventual winners, Australia.

Canada also made a notable breakthrough, making the quarter-finals after pool stage wins over Romania and Fiji. The Canadians' tournament ended in Lille with a 29-13 defeat by New Zealand.

1991 WORLD CUP STAT ATTACK

GROUP A			
N Zealand	18	England	12
Italy	30	USA	9
N Zealand	46	USA	6
England	36	Italy	6
England	37	USA	9
N Zealand	31	Italy	21

New Zealand and England qualify

GROUP B			
Scotland	47	Japan	9
Ireland	55	Zimbabwe	11
Ireland	32	Japan	16
Scotland	51	Zimbabwe	12
Scotland	24	Ireland	15
Japan	52	Zimbabwe	8

Scotland and Ireland qualify

GROUP C

Australia	32	Argentina	19
Wales	13	Western Samoa	16
Australia	9	Western Samoa	3
Wales	16	Argentina	7
Australia	38	Wales	3
Argentina	12	Western Samoa	35

Australia and Western Samoa qualify

GROUP D

France	30	Romania	3
Canada	13	Fiji	3
France	33	Fiji	9
Romania	11	Canada	19
Fiji	15	Romania	17
France	19	Canada	13

France and Canada qualify

QUARTER-FINALS

Scotland	28	Western Samoa	6
France	10	England	19
Ireland	18	Australia	19
Canada	13	N Zealand	29

SEMI-FINALS

| Scotland | 6 | England | 9 |
| Australia | 16 | N Zealand | 6 |

THIRD PLACE PLAY-OFF

| N Zealand 13 | Scotland | 6 |

WORLD CUP **FINAL**

| England | 6 | Australia | 12 |

1995
Uniting the Rainbow Nation

WHEN SOUTH AFRICA WERE readmitted into international rugby union in 1992 – after the sporting boycott caused by apartheid – it was pretty clear where the 1995 World Cup was going to be held. And for the first time it was to be staged in just one country.

BELOW An impressive view of the Kings Park Rugby Stadium, one of the venues for the 1995 World Cup in South Africa

The Rainbow Nation embraced the World Cup, creating a sensational tournament, which for South Africa had the perfect ending.

This Rugby World Cup was seen as the dawning of a new era, in a country where rugby meant so much. Not only was the political landscape changing but also rugby was on the very edge of the biggest change in its history, moving from an amateur sport to a professional one. Both came together in an incredible rugby tournament that captivated the world.

This World Cup went outside not only the boundaries of rugby, but of sport, as the new competition signalled the start of a new age in South Africa. A country defined for many decades by its politics was now defined by its sport.

The 1995 Rugby World Cup brought unforgettable images to the world

over the whole competition, scoring an incredible seven tries.

Unfortunately for England four of those tries came in a semi-final that no-one will ever forget.

Before the game England captain Will Carling called Lomu "a freak" and it clearly riled the All Black into action as he was over the line with just 70 seconds gone.

What followed for England was one of the worst quarters of rugby in their history and sent the Grand Slam champions crashing out of the World Cup.

In those sensational first 20 minutes New Zealand proceeded to score three tries, kick a penalty and have No 8, Zinzan Brooke, kick a drop goal, the first ever seen by a forward in international rugby.

The All Blacks went on to win 45-29, ensuring that England – who went on to lose the third-fourth place play-off match to France – conceded more points than at any other time in their international history.

LEFT Jonah Lomu breaks away from the tackle of England's skipper and captain, Will Carling, on his way to scoring a try in the semi-final, 1995

screen, from the arrival of the colossus, Jonah Lomu, to the image of South African President, Nelson Mandela handing over the Webb Ellis Cup to Springboks captain Francois Pienaar.

Mandela may have left us with the most endearing image but on the field the 1995 World Cup will be remembered for the world's first sighting of Lomu.

The 6ft 4in wing stood like a giant

South Africa had a far more conventional route into the final, beating France at rain-sodden Durban 19-15.

And it is fair to say that the final failed to live up to its billing. They are rarely classics but at least this one did make history as it became the first World Cup final to be settled in extra time.

New Zealand and South Africa were locked at 9-9 when the 80 minutes were completed, so up stepped Joel Stransky to win the game with an extra-time drop goal that sent the Rainbow Nation into raptures, with a 15-12 victory.

"No Hollywood scriptwriter could have written a better script," said Pienaar after receiving the Webb Ellis Cup from President Mandela.

"We didn't just have the support of 63,000 South Africans (in the ground) today. We had the support of 42 million South Africans (in the country).

"It was just unbelievable on the streets of South Africa. For the first time all the people had come together and all races and religions were hugging each other. It was just wonderful.

"At the final whistle I fell right to my knees. I'm a Christian and wanted to say a quick prayer for being in such a wonderful event, not because of the winning.

"Then all of a sudden I realised the whole team was around me which was a special moment."

And what about the moment when the cup was placed in your hands? "Nelson Mandela said 'thank you very much for what you've done for South Africa' but I said 'thank you for what you've done" recalled Pienaar "I almost felt like hugging him but it wasn't appropriate, I guess. Then I lifted the trophy, which was unbelievable. I can't describe the feeling as I wouldn't do it justice."

The one potentially sinister postscript came from the New Zealand team, where allegations of food poisoning surfaced, and the identity of a mystery waitress, 'Susie', who it was alleged was behind a plot to derail the

All Blacks' World Cup chances.

New Zealand coach Laurie Mains said: "It was just an amazing sequence of events and coincidence that, of our 35-man party that ate at that particular lunch venue in the hotel here, about 27 of them went down in the space of 12 hours.

"You can read what you like into that, but I don't think it was coincidence. We certainly have our suspicions."

A plot was never proved but a health problem – in the All Blacks camp – was not in doubt.

"We started falling over like flies, and that included 10 of the playing 15 and many of the other players and most of the management," added fly-half Andrew Mehrtens.

The tournament will be remembered, unfortunately, for more than the joy of the South African win as Ivory Coast wing Max Brito was paralysed after a tackle in the final Group D game against Tonga.

It was a tragic event in an otherwise joyful World Cup that for both Tonga and Ivory Coast ended with them being eliminated at the pool stage.

It was to be Ivory Coast's last appearance in a World Cup finals – to date – as

the second African place was taken by Namibia in 1999, 2003 and 2007.

The pool stages ended with a predictable quarter-final line-up, South Africa effectively taking Canada's place amongst the big boys, who were there in 1991.

Wales, after their failure to make the quarter-finals in 1991 following their defeat to Western Samoa, were forced to qualify this time around.

Wins over Romania and Italy ensured that Wales made it safely to South Africa but as a qualifier they were put in a tough group with both Ireland and New Zealand.

BELOW Tonga captain Manakaetau Otai breaks away during the match against the Ivory Coast, 1995

The All Blacks steamrollered over them and when they lost to Ireland by one point (24-23) they were destined to miss out on a place in the quarter-finals for the second successive tournament.

Western Samoa continued their development, beating Italy and Argentina for a quarter-final berth, where they lost to the host nation 42-14.

1995 WORLD CUP STAT ATTACK

GROUP A

South Africa	27	Australia	18
Canada	34	Romania	3
South Africa	21	Romania	3
Australia	27	Canada	11
Australia	42	Romania	3
South Africa	20	Canada	0

South Africa and Australia qualify

GROUP B

W Samoa	42	Italy	18
England	24	Argentina	18
W Samoa	32	Argentina	26
England	27	Italy	20
Italy	31	Argentina	25
England	44	W Samoa	22

England and Western Samoa qualify

GROUP C

Wales	57	Japan	10
N Zealand	43	Ireland	19
Ireland	50	Japan	28
N Zealand	34	Wales	9
N Zealand	145	Japan	17
Ireland	24	Wales	23

New Zealand and Ireland qualify

GROUP D

France	38	Tonga	10
Scotland	89	Ivory Coast	0
France	54	Ivory Coast	18
Scotland	41	Tonga	5
Tonga	29	Ivory Coast	11
France	22	Scotland	19

Scotland and France qualify

QUARTER-FINALS

France	36	Ireland	12
South Africa	42	W Samoa	14
England	25	Australia	22
N Zealand	48	Scotland	30

THIRD PLACE PLAY-OFF

| England | 9 | France | 19 |

SEMI-FINALS

| South Africa | 19 | France | 15 |
| N Zealand | 45 | England | 29 |

WORLD CUP **FINAL**

| South Africa | 15 | N Zealand | 12 |

1999
Wallabies clinch the double

THE QUALIFICATION PROCEDURES for the third World Cup were revamped with only the champions (South Africa), the runners-up (New Zealand) and the third place play-off winners (France) from 1995 going through as of right.

This forced giants like England into a qualification tournament, where they ran into Holland and Italy.

The qualification process didn't make a huge difference to the sides that made it through to the finals, although with 20 teams (up from 16) reaching the finals we saw tournament debuts for Spain, Uruguay and Namibia.

Uruguay won their 'minnows World Cup' with a 27-15 win over Spain in the first game, Uruguayan flanker Diego Ormaechea, becoming the oldest man – at 40 – to play in a match at the World Cup finals.

After a sensational tournament in 1995, the World Cup organisers unfortunately erred on a number of issues for this tournament and it certainly did not surpass the competition in South Africa.

RIGHT Diego Ormaechea of Uruguay scored his country's first try in the tournament to set them on the road to a 27-15 victory against Spain in 1999

Wales were the hosts but the biggest problem was in allowing matches to also be staged in Paris, Glasgow, Edinburgh, Twickenham, Dublin, Lens, Bordeaux, Huddersfield, Bristol, Toulouse, Beziers, Leicester, Limerick, Belfast and Galshiels.

Had the World Cup organisers learnt nothing from 1995 where the success was based around the tournament taking place in one nation? The marketing and promotion of the 1999 World Cup was a mess, and too many games were played in front of half-empty stadiums.

The increase in the number of teams to 20 was welcomed but the decision to divide those 20 teams into five pools of four teams was not.

While it meant one less pool match, the new system ensured the installation of a quarter-final play-off for six sides that failed to win their group. The games in the quarter-final play-off round were hopelessly timed shortly after the final pool match and too close to the actual quarter-finals.

The play-off system did allow Argentina to make a significant breakthrough and make their first quarter-final, after a victory over Ireland in Lens.

Gonzalo Quesada, who finished this World Cup as the leading scorer, was the hero with seven penalties and a conversion after Diego Albanese's late try.

The Pumas couldn't keep their run going in the last eight, losing 47-26 to France.

In any other World Cup, England would have moved into the quarter-finals by finishing second in their pool but in 1999 that was only good enough for a play-off against Fiji.

ABOVE English fullback Matt Perry (left) collides with New Zealand winger Jonah Lomu during the first-round match, 1999

ABOVE Jannie de Beer shows his kicking prowess. He is most famous for his world record five drop goals in a single match

away and I thought it was his day."

In truth, although England were knocked out by the South Africans, 44-21, it was their pool match defeat by New Zealand that actually destined them to an early exit.

Against New Zealand it was once again Jonah Lomu who came to haunt them, as the giant wing scored a 50-metre try, blasting through the English defence, as the All Blacks won 30-16. They couldn't hold Lomu in 1995 and it was the same story four years later.

That victory over England and a subsequent hammering of Scotland in the quarter-finals sent New Zealand into the last four as the hot favourites to claim their second world title.

But the All Blacks hadn't bargained for the unpredictability of the French, who staged the greatest comeback in World Cup history, to win 43-31.

In a semi-final played at Twickenham, France looked down and out when they went 24-10 behind to a side in magnificent form but upsetting the odds the French managed to score 33 points, with only seven from the All Blacks, to storm home.

"We let ourselves and our fans down and we are quite devastated,"

The fact that England won easily, 45-24, did little for their preparations for the last-eight clash with South Africa – in Paris – as it followed four days later. In that match Springbok fly-half Jannie De Beer kicked a world record five drop goals to help send England out.

"Jannie's was a truly phenomenal performance," said South Africa coach Nick Mallett.

"I told him before the game 'go out and have a bash'. He stuck one or two

said New Zealand coach John Hart, who subsequently lost his job. "The coach is accountable and I take full responsibility.

"We are a young side but that's no excuse. At 24-10, no way we should have lost."

In the other semi-final Stephen Larkham took Australia into the final with a dramatic drop-goal winner that stunned opponents South Africa, Matt Burke finishing them off with a late penalty.

"Stephen Larkham produced a wonder drop goal. When he did that there was pure elation, well on my behalf anyway, followed by a realisation we had to get back to it," said captain John Eales of the extra time victory.

"They were set to get right back out at us. But we managed to hold them off."

Australia duly won their second World Cup with a final 35-12 victory over France, at a tournament when defence was king. Australia in fact only conceded one try in the whole competition and that to a USA side – in a group game – after it was clear they were going to win.

"Straight after the game I turned to anyone who was there just to celebrate and go crazy," Eales added on BBC online.

"And then I realised I was going to get the trophy from the Queen. I thought "better make sure you don't swear" and after that was just really excited to represent the team and Australian rugby.

"I was filled with an immense satisfaction that we had achieved what we wanted to do – goals which had been set by some of us four years ago."

BELOW Stephen Larkham of Australia kicks a 40m drop-goal during the semi-final of the 1999 World Cup against South Africa

1999 WORLD CUP STAT ATTACK

GROUP A

Spain	15	Uruguay	27
Scotland	29	South Africa	46
Scotland	43	Uruguay	12
South Africa	47	Spain	3
South Africa	39	Uruguay	3
Scotland	48	Spain	0

South Africa and Scotland qualify

GROUP B

England	67	Italy	7
New Zealand	45	Tonga	9
England	16	New Zealand	30
Italy	25	Tonga	28
New Zealand	101	Italy	3
England	101	Tonga	10

England and New Zealand qualify

GROUP C

Fiji	67	Namibia	18
France	33	Canada	20
France	47	Namibia	13
Fiji	38	Canada	22
Canada	72	Namibia	11
France	28	Fiji	19

France and Fiji qualify

GROUP D

Wales	23	Argentina	18
Samoa	43	Japan	9
Wales	64	Japan	15
Argentina	32	Samoa	16
Wales	31	Samoa	38
Argentina	33	Japan	12

Wales and Argentina qualify

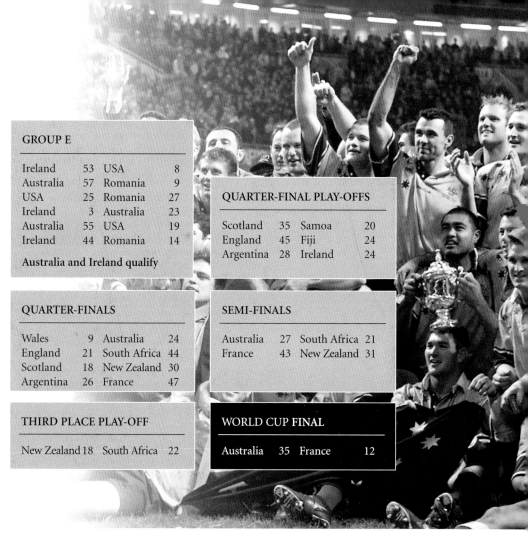

GROUP E

Ireland	53	USA	8
Australia	57	Romania	9
USA	25	Romania	27
Ireland	3	Australia	23
Australia	55	USA	19
Ireland	44	Romania	14

Australia and Ireland qualify

QUARTER-FINAL PLAY-OFFS

Scotland	35	Samoa	20
England	45	Fiji	24
Argentina	28	Ireland	24

QUARTER-FINALS

Wales	9	Australia	24
England	21	South Africa	44
Scotland	18	New Zealand	30
Argentina	26	France	47

SEMI-FINALS

| Australia | 27 | South Africa | 21 |
| France | 43 | New Zealand | 31 |

THIRD PLACE PLAY-OFF

| New Zealand | 18 | South Africa | 22 |

WORLD CUP FINAL

| Australia | 35 | France | 12 |

2003
Jonny gets England home

IT ONLY TOOK 16 YEARS, BUT finally – in 2003 – a side from the northern hemisphere won the Webb Ellis Cup: Clive Woodward's England.

The victory came in the most dramatic of styles. England and Australia locked together through 80 minutes of action and for a further 18 minutes of extra time they were separated only by an unforgettable drop goal by Jonny Wilkinson

Nine points behind at half-time, the Wallabies valiantly fought back through the boot of Elton Flatley to force extra time, before Wilkinson had the final word.

"It was a huge effort by the entire squad of players, coaches and backroom staff, everybody. Thanks to the fans, they were incredible," said England captain Martin Johnson.

"I can't say enough about the team,

RIGHT Nathan Sharpe charges through the Irish lines but his Australia side came up short in their attempt to retain the World Cup

OPPOSITE Wales' great performance against New Zealand in the group stages restored the belief in their abilities

because we had the lead and we lost it but we came back. And I can't say enough about Wilko at the end.

"I'm just happy for the players, they've put their heart and soul into it. It couldn't have been any closer and I'm just happy I'm on the right side."

Wilkinson was typically modest refusing – as usual – to take any praise despite winning it with that drop goal, scored with his weaker right foot.

"It was a massive team effort and a huge feeling of togetherness we had, certainly for the rest of the evening and through today as well," Wilkinson said. "It was an amazing feeling." Australia captain, George Gregan, was at his dignified best at the end, as he realised neither side could have done any more on a wonderful day for rugby.

"Congratulations must be extended to the English team, they delivered under pressure and they delivered when it counted," Gregan said.

"But I'm so proud of my guys. We gutsed it out, we fought back, we were down 14-5, we brought it back to extra-time." Woodward was the mastermind behind the victory and when he returned to England he was soon knighted.

From the moment England exited the 1999 tournament Woodward started a root and branch review of the England team, bringing in a plethora of specialist coaches and developing his team with a philosophy of trying to do 100 things one per cent better.

Not only did the Boks suffer on the pitch but off it as well as a video of naked players at their pre-World Cup training camp was shown around the world.

"This was apartheid-style military training and was dehumanising for the players," said South Africa's sports minister Ngconde Balfour. "In discussion with the SARFU president I have expressed my total condemnation and disgust at elements of the camp."

After suffering in the 1990s, Wales continued their re-emergence on the World Cup stage, coming closest to knocking England out in a memorable quarter-final in Brisbane.

Wales led 10-3, three minutes into the second half, before Will Greenwood inspired an England comeback with a try, and Woodward's team never looked back.

"We're gutted we couldn't get up but we've come a long way and I can't say any more than that," Wales coach Steve Hansen said, after seeing his side outscore England three tries to one.

Wales had got their belief from a 53-37 defeat to New Zealand that saw them outgun the All Blacks for long periods, even leading 37-33 at the start of the second half.

"We've raised our performances week

It was also a tournament when two former world champions – New Zealand and South Africa – imploded in public.

New Zealand disappointed their legions of fans by losing their semi-final against Australia, under the coaching of John Mitchell, who paid for the failure with his job.

If the fall out was bad in New Zealand it was even worse in South Africa, where their quarter-final exit was the subject of ministerial questions.

The Springboks were beaten by England in the group stages and eventually lost 29-9 to New Zealand in the last eight, the first World Cup when they hadn't managed to make at least the semi-finals.

by week but this was one hurdle we couldn't get over and the guys are very disappointed with the result," said Wales captain Colin Charvis, after the defeat to England.

"We thought we had a good chance – especially going in at half-time – but unfortunately England were a bit too strong for us." Unfortunately for the sides outside the world's top 12 – and those who value the promotion of rugby as a global game – it was a World Cup that polarised the nations at the top and bottom of the rankings.

England hammered Uruguay 111-13 and Australia went a step further with a record score in the finals, beating Namibia 142-0.

The Wallabies ran in a record 22 tries, which did the World Cup little good. Twenty-four hours before, New Zealand had surpassed Australia's previous tournament record score with a 91-7 victory over Tonga.

The number of huge scores led to a predictable quarter-final line-up, Fiji coming closest to breaking into the party, although they fell to Scotland, 22-20, in the group decider.

The Fijians did uncover one world star in the almost unstoppable Rupeni Caucaunibuca. He scored two tries in the game against Scotland but Tom Smith's score two minutes from time sent the Scots through.

With stars like Caucaunibuca, Wilkinson and Gregan on parade, the 2003 tournament was hailed as the best

BELOW Jonny Wilkinson was England's hero in the final, kicking a last-minute drop goal to win the World Cup

ever, with almost two million spectators – in ten cities – going through the turnstiles, to watch the 48 games, across 44 days.

More than 40,000 overseas visitors arrived in Australia for the tournament as once again the organisers decided to stage the World Cup in just one country.

But what made the tournament so special was the way it was embraced by the Australian people, who not only flocked to the big games but ensured there was a great atmosphere at the small clashes, like when Romania took on Namibia in Launceston.

"We were absolutely delighted with it. It has taken it to a new level," said Syd Millar, chairman of the International Rugby Board.

2003 WORLD CUP STAT ATTACK

GROUP A

Australia	24	Argentina	8
Ireland	45	Romania	17
Argentina	67	Namibia	14
Australia	90	Romania	8
Ireland	64	Namibia	7
Argentina	50	Romania	3
Australia	142	Namibia	0
Argentina	15	Ireland	16
Namibia	7	Romania	37
Australia	17	Ireland	16

Australia and Ireland qualify

GROUP B

France	61	Fiji	18
Scotland	32	Japan	11
Fiji	19	USA	18
France	51	Japan	29
Scotland	39	USA	15
Fiji	41	Japan	13
France	51	Scotland	9
Japan	26	USA	39
France	41	USA	14
Scotland	22	Fiji	20

France and Scotland qualify

GROUP C

South Africa	72	Uruguay	6
England	84	Georgia	6
Samoa	60	Uruguay	13
South Africa	6	England	25
Georgia	9	Samoa	46
South Africa	46	Georgia	19
Samoa	22	England	35
Georgia	12	Uruguay	24
South Africa	60	Samoa	10
England	111	Uruguay	13

England and South Africa qualify

GROUP D

N Zealand	70	Italy	7
Wales	41	Canada	10
Italy	36	Tonga	12
N Zealand	68	Canada	6
Tonga	20	Wales	27
Canada	14	Italy	19
N Zealand	91	Tonga	7
Italy	15	Wales	27
Canada	24	Tonga	7
N Zealand	53	Wales	37

New Zealand and Wales qualify

QUARTER-FINALS

N Zealand	29	South Africa	9
Australia	33	Scotland	16
France	43	Ireland	21
England	28	Wales	17

SEMI-FINALS

| N Zealand | 10 | Australia | 22 |
| England | 24 | France | 7 |

THIRD PLACE PLAY-OFF

| France | 13 | N Zealand | 40 |

WORLD CUP **FINAL**

| Australia | 17 | England | 20 |

Chapter 3

A – Z of the Rugby World Cup

A – Australia

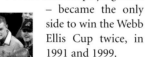

THE COUNTRY WITH THE MOST successful World Cup record – despite having one of the smallest playing bases – became the only side to win the Webb Ellis Cup twice, in 1991 and 1999.

After losing a very disappointing third-fourth play-off in 1987, Australia certainly didn't arrive at the 1991 tournament as one of the favourites. But they still had the nucleus of their 1984 Grand Slam side, and used that as their key to victory. The seminal game in 1991 came in the quarter-final when they looked down and out – in Dublin – after Gordon Hamilton scored a late try, which looked to have won the game. But stand-in captain Michael Lynagh replied with a length of the field move that took Australia into the semis. "That game – against Ireland – was the most emotional time of my life," remembered Australia captain Nick Farr-Jones. "It was similar to the birth of one of my children crammed into about four minutes.

"I'd like to think had I been on the field we wouldn't have been in that posi-

BELOW Australian players pose with the trophy after the 1999 final game

LEFT Nick Farr-Jones lifts the Rugby World Cup after their victory in the 1991 World Cup final

Australia crashed out in the 1995 World Cup to England in a quarter-final won in the dying seconds by a Rob Andrew drop goal but in 1999 with a new generation of players in the side they dominated the tournament, conceding just one try, and that was against the USA – in a pool game – when they had rested the majority of their front-line players. The final victory was the biggest in World Cup history with Australia trouncing the French 35-12.

It was the tournament where defence ruled the world, the Wallabies' almost watertight last line winning the day.

"The All Blacks were the favourites, the Springboks were defending champions and England were the great local hope," said Australia captain John Eales.

"As it turned out none of those teams made the final – it was us, and our mental focus had to be really strong. I was filled with an immense satisfaction that we had achieved what we wanted to do – goals which had been set by some of us four years ago."

Australia failed to become the first side to retain the Webb Ellis Cup. On home soil – in 2003 – they lost in extra time to a last-gasp drop goal from Jonny Wilkinson.

tion but when Gordon Hamilton scored, Michael Lynagh treated the situation very differently to how I would.

"I would have read the riot act but Michael asked the ref how long was left and then said he would kick long. That took guts and the rest is history as he went on to score. For sure we were lucky. One minute we were down and out of the World Cup and the next we were somehow back in it and on our way to face New Zealand."

B – Derek Bevan

THE REFEREE FROM Clydach, Derek Bevan, is part of an elite band of officials to take charge of a Rugby World Cup final, standing in the middle in 1991 as Australia beat England.

In 1995 Bevan was presented with a gold watch by South African president Louis Luyt at the end of the tournament as the best referee, even though Ed Morrison officiated in the final. Bevan was referee in South Africa's semi-final win over France.

Bevan was under huge pressure in that semi-final as a deluge meant the game was delayed 90 minutes and some thought it should have been delayed 24 hours, which would have caused huge problems for the World Cup organisers.

Bevan – who took up refereeing aged 25, after playing for Vardre – was among 17 Welsh International officials who received a traditional rugby 'cap' to mark their Test status at a special ceremony at the Millennium Stadium in 2006. By the end of the 2005-06 season there had been 54 referees from Wales who had controlled international matches and Bevan still holds the world record for the number of Tests he blew in – 44, over 15 years.

When Bevan – an electrical training officer – retired in 2000 he'd spent 26 years as a referee.

His last Test match was Ireland against Italy at Lansdowne Road.

"Derek quickly appreciated that the modern game demands a high level of fitness from all participants, including referees, so he changed his diet and upped his fitness training," said fellow Welsh referee Clive Norling.

"I know some people will find it hard to believe that referees also make friends but I regard that as the biggest bonus from doing something I have always enjoyed, with the good times far outweighing the bad," Bevan added.

The full line-up of World Cup Final referees.

1987	Kerry Fitzgerald (Australia)
1991	Derek Bevan (Wales)
1995	Ed Morrison (England)
1999	Andre Watson (South Africa)
2003	Andre Watson (South Africa)

C – Canada

ONE OF THE SIDES HURT MOST BY the advent of professionalism, Canada made a memorable World Cup quarter-final while the game was still amateur, in 1991. Victories over Romania and Fiji and only a six-point defeat to France, sent the Canadians through, where they were unfortunate to be paired with holders New Zealand, losing 29-13, in Lille, even though they outscored the All Blacks 10-8 in the second half. "We decided to do a lap of honour to say thanks to the French people who have given us such wonderful support here," recalled Canada captain Mark Wyatt.

Canada's hopes of following up their last eight place in 1991 with another one in 1995 were almost extinguished by the draw. Not only were they placed in the same group as hosts – and one of the favourites – South Africa but with the holders, Australia. Canada in fact came very close

to upsetting South Africa in an explosive final group match, where victory would have sent the Canadians through. The game boiled over with two Canadians – Rod Snow and Gareth Rees – and one South African – James Dalton – sent off following a brawl. Two other players – Scott Stewart of Canada and Pieter Hendricks of the South Africa – were later cited and banned as Canada crashed out under a 20-0 defeat.

BELOW Canada made the quarter-finals in 1991, losing to New Zealand

D – Jannie de Beer

ENGLAND WENT INTO THE 1999 World Cup quarter-final, against South Africa, as the underdogs. South Africa were the holders and England had been forced into a quarter-final play-off match four days before. Pundits expected them to lose but no one predicted the way they would lose, going out to a record-breaking feat from Springboks fly-half Jannie de Beer. The South African No 10 kicked an incredible five drop goals – in a 34-point haul – at the Stade de France. Far and away a world record. No side in the history of the World Cup had played with such a game plan, using the drop goal as their most potent weapon. De Beer was the executioner as the Springboks – and particularly centre Pieter Muller – worked themselves into positions to give their outside-half the chances he needed. "There was something supernatural happening out there, I definitely believe that," De Beer said. "I believe in my heart that victory was not just about the efforts of the

BELOW Jannie de Beer kicks his fourth drop goal against England in a quarter-final match, 1999

players. I feel God had a hand in this.

"I want to give him the glory. It was he who gave us the talent. You can plan up to a point, but there are just some things that happen that you don't have answers for. "Some of the things that happened on that pitch I don't have answers for. I gave my heart to the Lord in '93 and ever since that time, whenever I do anything, it's to glorify him.

"I have an individual relationship with Jesus Christ. I know he is my saviour and if things happen to me it's not by coincidence or because of my own brilliance. "You can win a World Cup but if you don't have Jesus Christ you don't have anything." De Beer failed to continue his incredible form into the semi-finals where – ironically – Stephen Larkham booted a drop goal to put Australia into the final, and knock South Africa out.

"I made a prediction that he would get three drop goals but I didn't expect five," said South Africa coach Nick Mallett.

"When somebody doesn't miss a kick all game and gets five out of five drop goals it's a special performance.

"You can't defend against drop goals," Woodward added. "I have never seen five drop goals in a game, especially one of this importance."

E – Eden Park

THE MAGNIFICENT STADIUM IN Auckland, New Zealand where the first Rugby World Cup Final was held and where it will return in 2011. The ground has hosted both rugby Test matches and cricket Test matches. Plans are in place to upgrade the famous stadium from its 47,500 capacity to 60,000 in time to host the 2011 World Cup final, and it also planned to use it as the venue for the opening match. The redevelopment includes a new three-tier South stand that will replace the old South and South West stands with a capacity of 24,000 and a new three-tier East stand, taking the number of covered seats from 23,000 to 38,000. The changes will also make sure the ground will have an International Cricket Council-compliant oval for the first time, although a proposal to build a roof – like the one at the Millennium Stadium – was rejected due to costs.

"Our bid promised an expanded, upgraded Eden Park to host the opening match and Final of the Rugby World Cup, with facilities and services fitting for such an event. This design concept will achieve that vision, as well as leaving a

ABOVE An aerial view of Eden Park which will be one of the venues for the 2011 World Cup

lasting legacy," explained Rugby World Cup 2011 Establishment Board chairman Jock Hobbs.

"Our goal is to showcase our country, our passion for rugby, and stage a world-class event."

Eden Park has been a sports ground since 1900, the Auckland Rugby Union leasing the Park in 1914, allowing it to become the home of Auckland Rugby in 1925.

In 1926 Eden Park was put in a Trust (Eden Park Trust Board) that provided for the Trustees to manage the Park primarily for the benefit of Auckland Cricket and Rugby. The first rugby Test match was staged in 1921 when the All Blacks beat South Africa 9-5.

ABOVE France, at the 1987 World Cup

OPPOSITE A lone France fan celebrates his side's amazing 43-31 win against New Zealand in 1999

F – France

THE MOST SUCCESSFUL NORTHERN hemisphere nation – on the world stage – they have made at least the semi-final in four out of five Rugby World Cup tournaments, since losing to New Zealand in the final, in 1987. Their affinity with the competition is also reflected in the fact that they have staged pool matches in two tournaments, in 1991 and 1999, and in 2007 will be the hosts, staging the final at the magnificent Stade de France at the end of October. Their best performance was in 1987 when they reached their first final with players like Serge Blanco, Philippe Sella and Didier Camberabero in their pomp. At that tournament they beat Australia 30-24 in the semi-final, coming from behind three times, the final time a try from Blanco going down in history as one of the best in World Cup history.

France staged one of the biggest shocks in World Cup history in 1999 when they upset hot favourites New Zealand – at Twickenham – in the semi-final. In an unforgettable game France slipped 24-10 behind but then proceeded to score 33 points to seven from the All Blacks, in a display that summed up everything good about French rugby. "France's stunning win over the All Blacks was the sporting equivalent of the Titanic getting the better of the iceberg, the sledgehammer losing to the nut," exclaimed Rob Kitson in The Guardian. "For a World Cup in danger of toppling off its narrow ridge on the cliff-face of international affairs, it was almost too good to be true. When Bill McLaren describes Sunday's spectacular as the greatest game of rugby he has ever seen, there can be simply no doubting France's achievement."

G – Georgia

AFTER RUGBY TURNED PROFESSIONAL in 1995 great efforts were made to ensure it wasn't a case of the rich (unions) getting richer and the poor unions getting poorer. So it was with great joy across the rugby world when Georgia emerged from Europe to qualify for the 2003 World Cup.

Their qualification was a massive spectacle in Georgia with 45,000 people converging on the National Stadium with around one and half million people watching the match live on national television, as they beat Russia to go through.

The draw wasn't too kind to them, though as they were placed in the same group as England and South Africa.

But it was about the experience for the likeable Georgians. "We can say the Georgian baby was born in Australia because in World Cup history whenever we take part in the future the media guides will say 'first participation: Australia 2003'," explained Georgia Rugby Union vice president Zaza Kassachvili.

BELOW Georgia players line up before the Rugby World Cup qualifier against Portugal, November 2006

"So we say Georgian rugby was born with a Georgian father and French mother with godmother Australia and godfather England because our first World Cup game was against England.

"We know it is a baby now, but the baby can be growing. It just needs the parents to be thinking about the baby and now we need in the next couple of years to be very attentive to this baby.

Kassachvili, who admitted the World Cup had been "like a big dream" has had to pinch himself to believe Georgia were playing in the Rugby World Cup, has already turned his attentions to the 2007 Tournament.

"We must be present in every World Cup now. We cannot go back, Georgia must be present. The place of Georgia is in the top 10 nations," Kassachvili added.

"It would be a big catastrophe if Georgia is not in the 2007 Rugby World Cup in France."

Georgia justified their participation in the 46-19 loss to South Africa, to come within 13 points at one stage. Hooker David Dadunashvili had the honour of scoring Georgia's first try at the World Cup finals. At game's end the Georgians were given a standing ovation as they jogged a lap of honour.

Georgia became the 18th country to qualify for the 2007 event enduring a torturous route to France, which ended with them beating Portugal in a two-legged contest, 28-11.

In Lisbon, Portugal improved from their display in Tblissi to draw 11-11, however the Georgians' 14-point lead (17-3) from the first leg books their World Cup place in Group D, alongside France, Ireland, Argentina and Namibia.

H – Humiliation

SHOCKS OR GIANT-KILLING ACTS are few and far between in the history of the World Cup but when they come they aren't forgotten. The first genuine shock came on 6 October, 1991 a date burned on the hearts of every Welsh rugby fan, the day a proud rugby nation lost to

BELOW 6 Oct 1991- the day that Wales were humiliated at Cardiff Arms Park when they lost to Western Samoa

Western Samoa on their very own Cardiff Arms Park ground.

Proving a point after not being invited to the 1987 World Cup, Western Samoa won 16-13, at Cardiff Arms Park.

"We feel it was quite unfair for us not to be invited last time because we were the South Pacific champions in 1987," said Samoan rugby supremo Tate Simi.

"We've proved a point to some degree this time by qualifying ahead of Tonga, but what we want to do now is show that we deserve to be in the

World Cup and not to have to go through the qualification rounds next time."

Samoa captain Peter Fatialofa called the three-point victory, "the greatest day in Samoan rugby history".

Wales captain Ieuan Evans was distressed. "We were devastated afterwards, and there were some pretty distraught fans there as well," he said.

"It showed how far we had deteriorated and let things slip, even if it took us another 10 years to do something about it.

"We probably got what we deserved after years of going through umpteen coaches and having a revolving-door policy with players. Not many people expected Wales to win the World Cup, but they didn't expect us to get knocked out at the pool stages.

"It was awful, horrible, something I wouldn't wish on my worst enemy."

The next big upset came in 1999 when odds-on favourites New Zealand, were knocked out at the semi-final stage by a rampant French team 43-31.

France were 24-10 behind before staging a comeback that stunned the rugby world, scoring 33 to seven from New Zealand, at Twickenham.

I – Ireland

IRELAND WERE ON THE WRONG end of their very own shock in 1999, when Argentina beat them in a quarter-final play-off that had the embarrassing repercussion of forcing them to qualify for the 2003 World Cup. "The Pumas exerted their normal squeeze up front and Ireland never looked comfortable," said Eddie Butler in The Observer. "Lansdowne Road would have been the place to be for a showdown with the French, but was not so attractive when it came to Argentina against France. It was a cultural and commercial opportunity lost. The Irish blew it."

They haven't always blown it but it is safe to say that Ireland have never over-achieved at the World Cup. Quarter-finalists in 1987, 1991, 1995 and 2003, Australia and France knocking them out twice each, they have never gone on from there. France eliminated them in 1995 and 2003 and Australia in the opening two World Cup tournaments in 1987 and 1991. Ireland – who were early opponents of the concept of a World Cup - came closest to clearing the quarter-final hurdle when they came within a missed

David Humphreys' drop goal of winning their pool in 2003. When Humphreys' drop sailed wide – in the deciding match against Australia – they lost all chance of meeting Scotland in the last eight. Unfortunately for the Irish the 17-16 defeat to Australia pitted them into a quarter-final against a power-ful France side.

"We are a devastated team at the moment," said the Ireland coach Eddie O'Sullivan after losing to Australia.

"We played all the rugby in the second half and deserved to win that game.

"But I am very proud of what they achieved, playing the world champions in their own back yard and taking the game to them every step of the way. If there was any justice we would have pulled that one off."

The France quarter-final, in 2003, which Ireland eventually lost 43-21 was the final act of one of Ireland's legends, Keith Wood, who ended the game embracing Fabien Galthie, another rugby warrior who knew he was retiring at the end of the 2003 World Cup.

ABOVE Brian O'Driscoll of Ireland chases a kick upfield during Ireland's quarter-final play-off against Argentina in 1999

BELOW Neil Jenkins kicks for goal during the match against Argentina played at his beloved Millennium Stadium in 1999

J – Neil Jenkins

KNOWN ACROSS THE WORLD AS the greatest points-scorer in the history of rugby, Neil Jenkins was lucky enough to become the world's most prolific points-scorer, not only in the World Cup but at his beloved Millennium Stadium. Jenks wasn't always the darling of the Welsh fans, having to fill a No 10 jersey occupied by players like Barry John, Phil Bennett and Cliff Morgan, but no-one could argue with his point-scoring. Before Jenkins, Michael Lynagh was the world's leading points-scorer with 911 for the Wallabies, but the man from Church Village rewrote the record books. He broke Lynagh's record in a pool game – in 2003 – against Samoa. Perhaps nervous early on he hit a post with a penalty, before

a conversion – to put Wales 7-3 ahead – took him past Lynagh's mark.

"I'm more concerned about the team," said Jenkins. "If the team scores four or five tries and I don't kick any kicks and we win, I'll be happier than if I get the points and we lose.

"All that matters is how well we do in this World Cup, not what records I might break."

Wales coach Graham Henry added: "I've coached for 27 years and you see a lot of very committed professionals and Neil Jenkins is right up there with the best of them.

"He's a role model for young rugby players, he deserves all the credit he gets.

"He's put hours and hours and hours of practice in and that's made him the best goalkicker in the world at the moment. And he plays a vital role in guiding our team."

Jenkins, who made his Wales debut at 19, certainly wasn't finished in the record-breaking department knocking over 44 consecutive kicks at goal for the Celtic Warriors in the 2003-04 season.

He ended his career with 87 caps and 1,049 points, the first player to go through the 1,000-point mark.

K – John Kendall-Carpenter

THE SOMERSET HEADMASTER was one of the key driving forces behind the establishment of the Rugby World Cup when many nations were sceptical about starting a competition that they believed would lead to the abandonment of the game's amateur ethos. He was the English representative on the International Rugby Board when they agreed to host the first World Cup, in 1987. He was appointed the chairman of the steering committee to oversee the World Cup and was crucial in the structuring of rugby's new tournament.

Kendall-Carpenter spent a lifetime devoted to rugby and, before becoming instrumental in the birth of the World Cup, played for England 23 times and was president of the Rugby Football Union as well as chairman of the International Board. A proud Cornishman, at the time of his death he was involved in the 1991 World Cup.

LEFT John Kendall-Carpenter in 1989 During his playing years, he won 23 England caps

L – John and Martin Leslie

THE LESLIE BROTHERS WERE TWO of the most famous Kilted Kiwis and part of a long line of players who were born in one country, but represented another in the World Cup. The Leslies were born in New Zealand, qualifying for the Scotland team through their Scottish father.

The arrival of the Kilted Kiwis didn't receive universal approval, with former captain David Sole, believing it was a backward move to bring in players to the Scotland team who weren't born there.

"It was interesting in the way they arrived. I was surprised and at a loss as to how they came to fly across to Scotland and make their homes here," said Sole.

"And I was doubly surprised when John Leslie got the captaincy. I don't think there is any question about his capability as a player but it was very strange to appoint him captain.

"I think the Leslies would say, hand on heart, that they would love to play for New Zealand.

"We've gone too far to the opposite end of the scale where we are looking for rugby mercenaries."

But John Leslie, who scored a Six Nations try in

BELOW Martin Leslie in action during the first-round match between Scotland and Uruguay, 1999

just over nine seconds, against Wales retorted: "Leave the boys alone. We don't make up the rules. The critics are not looking at the whole picture. If they don't like it, they should change the rules.

"It became a personal thing – I felt persecuted by it. I don't need it. I'm just trying to do my best for whoever picks me."

Some other notable World Cup players who represented a country in which they weren't born include:

Mike Catt (England): South Africa
George Gregan (Australia): Zambia
Simon Shaw (England): Kenya
Victor Ubogu (England): Nigeria
Serge Betsen (France): Cameroon
Serge Blanco (France): Venezuela
Pieter De Villiers (France): South Africa
Marc Livremont (France): Senegal
Frankie Sheahan (Ireland): Canada
Dafydd James (Wales): Zambia

M – Nelson Mandela

BELOW Nelson Mandela waves to the crowd after his country won the World Cup

THERE ARE FEW MORE ENDEARING images in the history of sport - let alone rugby – than the one of South African President Nelson Mandela at the 1995 World Cup final. On 24 June, dressed in a green Springboks jersey – resplendent with a number six on the back – he appeared to present the Webb Ellis Cup to South Africa captain Francois Pienaar with an air of dignity and majesty that perhaps only he could have delivered. It is the photograph with which most rugby fans associate the Rugby World Cup and especially that magical tournament in 1995. The Rainbow Nation was in its infancy at that point but the handshake did so much for the country as a whole, coming as it did after an incredibly tense final, won in extra time by a Joel Stransky drop goal.

In Pienaar's book, Rainbow Warrior, he recounts perfectly the moment when the rugby world stood still.

"Then when President Mandela came out to present the Cup there was a hell of a lump in my throat," said Piennar. 'I wasn't aware that he was going to wear my shirt. When he handed me the Cup he said, 'Thank you very much for what you've done for South Africa.' And I said 'No, you've got it wrong. Actually, it's what you've done.'

"Sport in general has got the ability to be a unifier, not only in South Africa, but all over the world. Sport has got that mystique, it's such a powerful tool."

Mandela's love affair with rugby didn't end in 1995 and he has attended a number of Test matches since, the Springboks wearing his old prison number, 46664, on their shirts.

And New Zealand coach Steve Hansen even felt it contributed to a better performance from the Springboks.

"They brought out old 46664 again, and he's as good as any drug you can get over there," said Hansen.

"They just find another leg and another arm - and so they should; he's not man of the century for nothing."

N – New Zealand

THE NEW ZEALAND ALL BLACKS have perfected the skill of being the best team in the world, in years when there isn't a World Cup! Winners at the first tournament – in 1987 – it is incredible to think that such a great rugby nation had to wait at least 20 years to get their hands on the Webb Ellis Cup again. But they have stood over the World Cup like a colossus since it kicked off. Even though they haven't managed to win it since 1987 they have never failed to make at least the semi-finals, while losing in the 1995 final to a Joel Stransky drop goal. It was probably in 1995 when they came into the tournament as hottest favourites. The 1993 Lions were vanquished and with Jonah Lomu on board they headed for the 1995 World Cup in irresistible form. But they hadn't bargained for hosts South Africa – not to mention Nelson Mandela – being behind them. They may not have dominated at World Cups but in Tri-Nations games since 1996 the All Blacks have won almost double the number of victories obtained by Australia, yet in the same period the Wallabies have won a World Cup (1999) and made the final four years later. No side in the rugby world has a positive record (ie more wins than losses) against New Zealand and there are some 'big' rugby nations like Ireland and Scotland who have never beaten them. Their worst record is against their oldest foes, South Africa, but they have still won 38 of their contests, compared to 29 for South Africa.

ABOVE David Kirk holds up the Webb Ellis Cup after New Zealand beat France in the 1987 World Cup

Successive New Zealand coaches have never managed to work out why that record has not been translated into World Cup victories. The only thing that is certain is World Cup failure (ie not to win it) means the end of a particular coach's regime, as happened to John Hart in 1999 and John Mitchell in 2003.

ABOVE Diego Ormaechea (top) qtackles Scottish fullback Glenn Metcalfe during the World Cup first-round match, 1999

O – Diego Ormaechea

THE 40-YEAR-OLD VETERINARY surgeon from Uruguay arrived at the 1999 World Cup as the oldest player ever to take part in the finals. Ormaechea was an inspiration to his side, leading them to a fabulous victory over Spain, 27-15, at Galashiels. When Ormaechea made his World Cup debut he'd been representing his country for 20 years and in fact scored their first try – from the back row – against Spain, in the battle of the 1999 minnows. Ormaechea made his debut in 1979 and in 1999 was amazed to be playing at a Rugby World Cup.

"This is not something I ever believed could happen," he said. "To be here is a dream come true at the end of my career and I am enjoying everything.

"It was good to be here, but to win our first match was even better. To score was an unbelievable moment for me. It opened the way for victory and rewarded the efforts made by the whole team.

"We don't get anything (money) for being here. We're from another world."

Ormaechea played his last Test in the 1999 pool, 39-3, defeat to South Africa and almost inevitably went on to become Uruguay's coach, taking them to the next World Cup, in 2003.

"It's a success for us just to be here," said Ormaechea, the coach, in 2003.

P – Pool System

EVER SINCE THE EMERGENCE OF the Rugby World Cup in 1987 they have persisted with a pool-based system to determine qualification for the knock-out rounds. But with the first World Cup being contested by 16 teams and the 2007 featuring 20, the organisers have tinkered with the way those pools have operated. The worst system was concocted for the 1999 tournament as the Rugby World Cup organisers decided – inexplicably – to divide the 20 teams into five groups of four. This meant the group leaders went through, as of right, the best runner-up joined them and then the six next best sides were sent into a new round: the quarter-final play-offs. The system was a disaster because the play-off winners were then forced to play a quarter-final four days later and unsurprisingly all the play-off winners went out at the next stage, all hammered. Luckily sanity returned in 2003 when we returned to four groups of five, with the top two sides going through to the last eight. Bonus points were also introduced in 2003 with sides getting four points for a win and bonus points

awarded for sides scoring four tries or more and for sides who lose by seven points or less. The bonus point system made no difference to the sides that actually qualified for the quarter-finals but it is a system adopted throughout the rugby world, to encourage attacking play. France and New Zealand were the only sides – in 2003 – to pick up a maximum of four bonus points, while qualifying.

BELOW Joost van der Westhuizen of South Africa passes to Percy Montgomery (15) in the 1999 Rugby World Cup quarter-final match against England

Q – Gonzalo Quesada

NOT MANY ARGENTINEANS HOLD World Cup records but prolific goal-kicker Gonzalo Quesada is certainly an exception, scoring an impressive 102 points at the 1999 World Cup, one more than the nearest player, Matt Burke. Quesada's impressive kicking display was one of the main reasons for Argentina's breakthrough in 1999, as they made the quarter-finals for the first time. And Quesada's achievement is all the more remarkable considering the fact that Burke's Australia stayed in for an additional two rounds. In 1999 Quesada – who won 36 caps for The Pumas – raised a few eyebrows as he rejected the use of a kicking tee, instead opting for sand to play the ball on.

"Each time I am using a tee, I feel I am limiting my possibility to give the ball the orientation that I want," said Quesada, who also scored 33 points at the 2003 World Cup, before retiring from Test rugby after that tournament. "With the sand I can mould my support how I want and choose my height with more or less sand. Each time I have used a tee I have missed my kick, but I will continue to train with them, if others can manage to do it. Why not me?"

He was nicknamed Speedy Gonzalo because of the time he took to take his kicks at goal, something that was restricted at the World Cup, as a 60-second limit for kicks at goal was introduced.

RIGHT Gonzalo Quesada kicks for goal during the World Cup Pool D match between Argentina and Samoa in 1999

R – Huw Richards

THE WELSHMAN HAD THE unenviable distinction of becoming the first player to be sent off in a World Cup match when he was dismissed in the 1987 semi-final against New Zealand. Wales were demolished in the game, as New Zealand were unstoppable, winning 49-6. It was one of the few occasions on which a sending-off had little or no bearing on a Test match. Richards was shown the red card by Kerry Fitzgerald, the Australian referee, in the final minutes of the game for punching Gary Whetton. The punch caused a brawl and the unfortunate Richards was then knocked semi-conscious by All Blacks No 8 Wayne Shelford who should have been – but was not – dismissed as well. Sendings-off followed Wales around in that tournament and when they beat Australia 22-21 in the following game, to win the third-fourth play-off, David Codey of Australia was also dismissed. Richards and Codey were not of course the last men to be sent off at a World Cup finals and in the next four World Cups a further 11 players saw red, but none in 2003.

The full list of World Cup sinners is:

1987 **Huw Richards:**
   For Wales against New Zealand
   David Codey:
   For Australia against Wales
1991 **Pedro Sporleder:**
   For Argentina against W.Samoa
   Mata'afa Keenan:
   For W.Samoa against Argentina
1995 **James Dalton:**
   For South Africa against Canada
   Gareth Rees:
   For Canada against South Africa
   Rod Snow:
   For Canada against South Africa
   Feleti Mahoni:
   For Tonga against France
1999 **Marika Vunibaka:**
   For Fiji against Canada
   Dan Baugh:
   For Canada against Namibia
   N Ta'ufo'ou:
   For Tonga against England
   Brendan Venter:
   For South Africa against Uruguay
2003 None

Courtesy of The IRB Yearbook

ABOVE Mataafa Keenan of Western Samoa is sent off in the match against Argentina during the 1991 World Cup

S - South Africa

THE SOUTH AFRICANS HAD THE distinction of being one of the nations that voted for the establishment of a World Cup – in 1985 – in the knowledge they would not be allowed to take part. Their enthusiasm could probably be attributed to the success they had enjoyed since arriving on the Test scene in the 1920s, only losing on a regular basis to the New Zealand All Blacks. The sporting boycott caused by South Africa's apartheid political regime meant that the Springboks missed the 1987 and 1991 World Cups but they were back with a bang in 1995. South Africa were finally readmitted to international rugby

in 1992 with an historic Test against New Zealand in Johannesburg on 15 August and it wasn't long before the International Rugby Board was awarding the third World Cup to the Rainbow Nation. The All Blacks came into the tournament as the undisputed world's number one side but they had managed to peak in between World Cups. The South African form was far from conclusive in the opening rounds and they only scraped into the final after beating France in a rain-sodden semi-final in Durban. But once they made the final it was as if the gods of rugby had conspired in their favour. Even though the All Blacks had hammered England in their semi-final and had the seemingly unstoppable Jonah Lomu in their ranks, the Springboks triumphed. It took them until extra time to do so, Joel Stransky kicking the unforgettable drop goal to hand them a 15-12 victory. A nation – and perhaps a continent – celebrated! Many South Africans felt they would go on from this to dominate international rugby but they lost a thrilling semi-final to Australia in 1999 and four years later bowed out at the quarter-final stage, losing to New Zealand after being beaten by England in the pool stages.

BELOW South African fans enjoy the opening ceremony of the 1995 World Cup prior to their team's opening match against Australia

T- Television

BROADCASTERS HAVE ENJOYED A huge influence over the game of rugby union and at the World Cup, often dictating the kick off times of matches. But the coverage in the media has been crucial to the development of the tournament, which started when the sport of rugby union was a strictly amateur affair.

The first tournament – in 1987 – was light years away from the event in 2003. In 1987 600,000 people passed through the turnstiles with 300 million in 17 countries watching the action on television. By 2003 two million spectators attended the matches (average of 38,282 per game) during the Rugby World Cup, watched by a cumulative world television audience of 3.5 billion, broadcast in 205 countries. This included 400 jumbos of international tourists and 500,000 Australian bed nights giving plenty of rest to the 40,000 overseas visitors.

The internet grew during the course of the tournament. Few companies had websites in 1987 but by 2003 rugbyworldcup.com had 495 million hits over the Tournament including 44.5 million hits on the day of the Final.

The Rugby World Cup is now established as the third biggest sporting event behind the Olympic Games and FIFA World Cup, although the sport failed in its campaign to gain admission to the Olympic Games, for the 2012 event in London.

In 2003 ITV was the host broadcaster in the UK, showing over 200 hours of programming, the majority live. Every one of the 48 matches were shown live on ITV1 or ITV2.

U – The Underwoods

TWO OF THE MOST FAMOUS brothers to play in the World Cup, Tony and Rory Underwood enjoyed varying degrees of success for England in the 1990s when both were Test players. Rory was always the senior partner of the double act – not just in age – and had a prolific record for England at World Cups running in 11 tries.

Rory's full England career brought a remarkable 49 tries in 85 Tests, and he was made an MBE in 1992 for his services to rugby.

The Underwood brothers were the first to play in the same England team together since 1937 when they started against South Africa in 1992, in a 33-16 win for England, Tony scoring a try.

Rory certainly had the more memorable of World Cup careers, making his debut in 1987, excelling at the tournament four years later, and ending his career in 1995.

Rory was robbed of the chance to win the World Cup for England in 1991, David Campese knocking on, perhaps deliber-

CENTRE Rory and Tony Underwood were the first brothers to represent England at the same time since 1937

ately, a pass from Peter Winterbottom to Underwood, that if caught would have given the wing a clear run to the line.

Tony in contrast is hardly likely to forget his only World Cup campaign – in 1995 – but probably for the wrong reasons.

Tony was selected for the semi-final, in Cape Town, and asked to mark the

"I was feeling fairly confident. I'd played well all season and scored a try in the win over Australia, so I was hardly going to say: 'I can't handle Jonah.'

"The only saving grace I can take from the whole thing is that I wasn't steamrolled by Jonah for his four tries. Sadly that happened to all my team-mates after I got caught out of position."

In that semi-final Tony's brother Rory restored some family pride with two tries in the game to ensure some respectability to the scoreline.

The 2003 World Cup featured nine sets of brothers, including twins, some playing for different countries. Dimitri and Gregoire Yachvili represented France and World Cup debutants Georgia respectively, while Brent and Matt Cockbain were in the squads of Wales and Australia.

colossus that is Jonah Lomu.

It is fair to say that Lomu won that battle, scoring four tries and throwing Underwood – like a rag doll – off the field at one point.

"I remember Jack Rowell (coach) and Will Carling (captain) asking me if I could handle Jonah on my own," Underwood recalls.

Another set of siblings who played for different countries at RWC 2003 were Rodney and Steven So'oialo, who represent New Zealand and Samoa respectively.

Argentina had two sets of brothers in their ranks – in 2003 – in twins Felipe and Manuel Contepomi and Juan de la Cruz Fernández Miranda and Nicolás Fernández Miranda.

V – Dr Roger Vanderfield

THE CHAIRMAN OF THE International Rugby Board in the 1980s, Dr Roger Vanderfield, was another man who was crucial to the establishment of the Rugby World Cup as one of the most important sports tournaments in the world. When the proposal for a World Cup arrived at the door of the IRB Dr Vanderfield's support was vital, as there were a number of dissenting voices in the rugby world. Vanderfield was an international referee, officiating in 15 Test matches between 1956 and 1974, ending his career in the middle with New Zealand's 16-6 victory over Australia in Sydney.

RIGHT New Zealand who will be the hosts for the 2011 World Cup

W – William Webb Ellis

THE RUGBY SCHOOL STUDENT IS credited with being the father of the game of rugby union, although there is little or no evidence to suggest that he actually "picked up the ball and ran with it" as legend tells us. The game certainly has its origins at Rugby School and many of its former pupils left an indelible mark on the history of the game, moving from country to country to help establish rugby. It is far more likely – according to Jed Smith, the eminent historian at the Museum of Rugby – that a group of Rugby schoolboys established the game, deriving rugby from one of the ball-based games already played at the school. Pupils would meet at the end of each day to discuss rules and how the game was developing. Webb Ellis's grave – in the south of France – has become something of a shrine and the heritage he brings to the game made his name the obvious choice for the World Cup trophy, which is called the Webb Ellis Cup. The cup – which is made of gilt silver – was made by Garrard and Co of London and modelled on a 1906 trophy made by Carrington and Co of London, designed by Paul de Lamerie.

The Australians gave it the nickname 'Bill' when they won it in 1991 and in 1999 they ran a 'Bring Back Bill' campaign.

The claim that Webb Ellis invented the game didn't appear until after his death, explaining how hard it was to corroborate, and in 1895 a Rugby School investigation turned up no evidence to support the theory that boys were allowed to play the game with their hands.

Rugby union was finally established as a credible sport in 1871 when a common set of laws was established at a meeting to form the Rugby Football Union, where there would clearly have been some former Rugby School pupils. The first international – against Scotland – followed soon after. In 1871 representatives from rugby clubs across the country met to form the Rugby Football Union and draw up their own common code of laws.

ABOVE The grave stone of William Webb Ellis with the Webb Ellis Cup on it at Menton Cemetery

ABOVE Lote Tuqiri who switched codes, moving from League to play Union with the Waratahs. He made his international debut for the Wallabies in 2003 against Ireland

X – Cross Coders

THROUGHOUT THE HISTORY OF rugby union the game has lost a significant number of players to the professional sport of rugby league. This changed in 1995 when union shed its amateur ethos, leading to a number of league players signing for union clubs. In the 2003 World Cup final former league players scored both tries, Lote Tuqiri getting the first for Australia and England's Jason Robinson diving over

in the corner to put his side back in the lead. With the dominance of league in Australia it isn't surprising that two other former league players – Mat Rogers and Wendell Sailor – also played for the Wallabies in that World Cup campaign. There were a number of other former league players dotted around the other teams at the tournament, most notably Wales outside-half Iestyn Harris. England also used former Great Britain coach Phil Larder as their defence coach in their successful 2003 campaign, and when he left the job in 2006 his place was taken by his former league colleague, Mike Ford.

Y – Youngest and other records

THE YOUNGEST PLAYER AT THE 2003 World Cup was Georgian scrum-half Merab Kvirikashvili who, at 19 was nearly half the age of the oldest player, Canadian captain Al Charron who, at 37 years and two months, was playing in his fourth Rugby World Cup. More than 10 other players were only 20 years old when Rugby World Cup 2003 kicked off on 10 October, including Wales forward Jonathan Thomas, Sailosi Tagicakibau of Samoa and USA Eagles flanker Todd Clever.

SA Eagles most-capped player Luke Gross and England's Simon Shaw were the tallest players on show at Rugby World Cup 2003 at 206cm, with Samoan fly-half Earl Va'a the shortest at 166cm.

Joeli Veitayaki, the Fijian prop, was the heaviest player at 136kg, some 66kg more than the lightest in Ireland scrum-half Peter Stringer.

And at the end of the 2003 tourna-

LEFT Fijian prop Joeli Veitayaki, the heaviest player in the World Cup at 136kg

ment a number of rugby greats called time on their careers, including: Fabien Galthie (France), Martin Johnson (England), Keith Wood (Ireland), Bryan Redpath (Scotland), Joost van der Westhuizen (South Africa), Al Charron (Canada), Rolando Martin (Argentina), and Waisale Serevi (Fiji).

BELOW Earl Va'a's team-mates tower over him

Z – Zimbabwe

AT THE 1987 WORLD CUP THE 16 competing nations were invited, rather than having to qualify. With South Africa subject to a sporting boycott due to the presence of the apartheid political regime in their country, an African substitute was sought and finally agreed as Zimbabwe, a position they held in 1991, although the side failed to win any matches in those first two World Cups. Once South Africa were readmitted in 1995, they were given the first African place and although a second African country is now admitted – as part of the qualification process – Zimbabwe have never made it. In 2006, Namibia qualified as the second African country for the third successive World Cup, Zimbabwe being eliminated, falling further down the pecking order – to 53rd in the world - than any of the 16 sides who competed in 1987.

Looking to the future, things look much brighter for Zimbabwe. Their Under-18 side qualified for the 2007 Under-19 World Championship with an impressive display at CAR's Africa Under-18 tournament in Morocco.

RIGHT Andy Ferreira of Zimbabwe passes out of the scrum in the game against Ireland, during the 1991 World Cup

Chapter 4

World Cup Stars

15 players who have lit up rugby's greatest show on earth

SERGE BLANCO
Country: *France*
Position: *Full-back / Wing*
Test Caps: *93*
Test Points: *233*
World Cups (2): *1987 and 1991*

IF ONE PLAYER SUMMED UP THE flair, spirit and general joie de vivre of the French rugby team in the 1970s and 80s, it was full-back Serge Blanco.

A 60-a-day smoker through his 12-year Test career, Blanco was grace personified – with a cheeky side – while a veritable brick wall as the last line of defence.

Perhaps the greatest player France ever produced, he scored one of the greatest tries the World Cup has even seen, when France beat Australia to reach the first World Cup final, in 1987.

The artisan of the French team in two World Cup campaigns, the first – in 1987 – where they made that final, Blanco left the World Cup with one of its most endearing memories.

"In that classic semi-final France launched a long, sweeping movement as only they can, involving forwards and all their backs," recalled The Observer's Eddie Butler.

"Serge Blanco had to finish it. The full-back had been complaining of hamstring trouble, but still mustered the speed to make it to the line at the corner, despite the tackle of the burly Wallaby hooker Tommy Lawton."

Unfortunately for Blanco and Les Bleus they couldn't finish the job by beating New Zealand in the final and by the time the 1991 tournament came around Blanco was captain.

Once again France fell short, this time suffering a far more unpalatable defeat, losing in the quarter-final to England, in Paris. Blanco retired once the tournament was over.

But even in his last game, even though France lost, he stayed in the headlines. Two minutes into the game Blanco landed a flurry of punches on England wing Nigel Heslop, who was late into a tackle.

"The referee warned me that I would go for another punch, but he said that he was a good friend of mine and it was his duty to see that I did not leave the field in that way," Blanco said.

Blanco, who was born in Venezuela, racked up a then world-record 38 tries in a career that started when he joined Biarritz in 1975.

"My game, such as it was, was 'instinctif, spirituel'," Blanco explained.

"I could not coach at any senior level: I have had my share of stress and ten-

ABOVE Serge Blanco dashes through the Welsh defence in 1991

OPPOSITE Blanco was a master with ball in hand and with the boot

sion caused by rugby, and I have seen it become even more pressurised and maniacal for coaches than even for the players themselves, the ones who are actually going out to perform."

One of the greatest full-backs the world has ever seen Blanco was quick enough to make his Test debut on the wing and play 11 more times there for France.

In a ground-breaking career he won 93 caps for France. After retiring Blanco stayed involved with his beloved Biarritz Olympique, eventually becoming the club president, presiding over their French Championship win in 2002 and their appearance in the 2006 Heineken Cup final, where they lost to Munster. Blanco also became the president of the French League.

DAVID CAMPESE

Country: *Australia*
Position: *Wing*
Test Caps: *101*
Test Points: *315*
World Cups (3): *1987, 1991 and 1995*

THE ULTIMATE SHOWMAN, DAVID Campese played in two Rugby World Cups, leaving an indelible mark on the 1991 tournament, where he was instrumental in Australia lifting the Webb Ellis Cup for the first time. His knock-on (whether deliberate or not) in the final certainly helped Australia to victory but it was in the semi-final where he showed his genius. Australia had won a heart-stopping victory against

BELOW David Campese makes a break during the 1991 Australia v New Zealand semi-final match

Ireland in the quarters and their reward was a clash with holders New Zealand. But when the going got tough, Campo took centre stage. Described by his captain in 1991, Nick Farr-Jones, as "pure genius" Campese took that semi-final by the scruff of its neck to knock the All Blacks out. Voted Player of the Tournament in 1991, the New Zealand game was unquestionably his finest in the green and gold. Campese had already scored tries against Argentina, Wales and Ireland and it only took him 12 minutes to cross the line against the All Blacks crossing from wing to first receiver and drifting over the line on the perfect angle and with the game just 35 minutes old he created a magnificent score for Tim Horan. Tearing through the New Zealand defence he threw an outrageous over the shoulder pass to Horan, and Australia were in the final. "There's always Campo, and when you've got a player like that in your team you always know probably something is going to happen," said All Blacks coach Alex Wylie. "He did it again – he just pulled that one out. An individual like that: one day he could probably blow it, but the other four days he could make it. It was just unfor-

tunate he made it against us."

Campese wasn't blessed with devastating speed but he possessed the guile to unlock any defence in the rugby world.

A motor-mouth of the highest order, Campese may not have scored in the 1991 final win over England but many credit him with convincing England to ditch their forward-dominated game plan for a more expansive outlook, which many consider was crucial to their downfall.

He didn't take long to announce himself on the world stage. Given his debut at nineteen against New Zealand in Christchurch he was handed the task of marking Stu Wilson, one of the world's best at the time.

"He left Wilson standing. He totally stood him up," explained Australia coach Bob Dwyer.

"At once we knew it was a very rare person we had on our hands. It wasn't the fact that he beat him, or even the way that he did, that was so stunning. It was that he had the daring to try it in the first place."

When Campese retired his 64 Test tries were a world record, overtaken in 2006 by Japan's Daisuke Ohata.

JOHN EALES

Country: *Australia*
Position: *Second row*
Test Caps: *86*
Test Points: *173*
World Cups (3): *1991, 1995 and 1999*

THROUGHOUT JOHN EALES'S 10-year reign in the Australia second row the man from Brisbane was called 'Nobody'.

Strange you may think for one of the most successful rugby players in the history of the game; a player who won every international honour available.

But you can understand where the moniker came from when you appreciate he was called 'Nobody' because, well…'Nobody is perfect'.

Perfection was a state that Eales achieved many times in his career. Certainly, no one could accuse him of being the archetypal second row.

Not only was he one of the world's best in the lineout and loose but he also scored a remarkable 173 points in Test matches, as he became an accomplished goalkicker. That total ensured he was the highest scoring forward in Test history.

Unfortunately for his opponents he was as happy winning the ball at the front of a lineout, in a scrum, ruck or in the backline making try-saving tackles. His athleticism set him apart from the majority of second-row forwards.

Eales also timed his retirement to perfection. In 2001, the season he helped Australia to a series win over the Lions, two years after their second World Cup victory, and while still at the top of his game, he made his announcement.

Eales agonised over the decision for some time but said: "At the end of the Lions series I sat back and reassessed my playing future and I decided that I would throw everything into this Tri-Nations campaign before stepping down for good."

His departure was felt throughout all Australian society and not just in the rugby world, prompting prime minister John Howard to say: "I wish to record my admiration for the magnificent contribution that John Eales has made to the game of rugby, and to Australian and international sport.

"John Eales has been an inspirational leader, an outstanding and courageous player, and an example to all in the way he has conducted himself on and off the field."

Off the field, Eales was awarded the Order of Australia Medal in 1999 for his services to rugby and the community.

His Test career started in 1991 – in Brisbane – against Wales and he ended after winning everything that was possible in the game: World Cup (twice), Tri-Nations, Bledisloe Cup and that series victory over the Lions.

At state level he played 112 times for Queensland, kicking off at the Brothers Rugby Club.

Australia won 41 of his record 55 Tests as captain following his appointment to the job, for the first time, in 1996.

Perhaps we should have guessed all those years ago that his was destined to be one of the most successful careers in the history of the game as the Wallabies won that first Test match by a record margin, 63-6. From then on the records just kept falling.

But of all those records that fell he must surely be proudest of his two World Cup victories.

Eales played in all of Australia's matches as they lifted the Webb Ellis Cup with a 12-6 defeat of England, in 1991. Playing more like a flanker he marauded around the field, the baby of the Wallabies' pack.

And eight years later Eales was there once again, but this time as the side's captain as they trounced France 35-12 in the final.

BELOW John Eales runs with the ball during a Tri-Nations match against South Africa.

GRANT FOX

Country: *New Zealand*
Position: *Outside-half*
Test Caps: *46*
Test Points: *645*
World Cups (2): *1987 and 1991*

BEHIND EVERY GREAT TEAM THERE is usually a great goalkicker. Think of England in 2003 and you see Jonny Wilkinson, Australia in 1991 and it is Michael Lynagh, and of course Joel Stransky is inextricably linked to the 1995 Springboks' World Cup win.

But standing above all those legendary goalkickers – in World Cup terms – is Grant James Fox, one of the key reasons why New Zealand ruled the rugby world in the late 1980s and early 1990s.

When New Zealand won the 1987 World Cup they scored 298 points in six matches, 126 of them by fly-half Fox. He scored 26 against Fiji and 17 in their 29-9 victory in the final against France. That 126-point total set a tournament record that still stands today.

Born in New Plymouth, Fox became a New Zealand legend after attending world famous Auckland Grammar School, and going on to set new standards, across the world.

In a mould-breaking 11-year career for Auckland and the All Blacks he kicked a remarkable 1,621 goals, at an incredible average of almost 14 points a game for both teams.

He was never an outside-half with the air of a Barry John or Phil Bennett but his radar boot could not be denied and he was in fact a far better runner than most people ever gave him credit for. His tactical kicking allied with his rugby brain delivered as many games for the All Blacks as his almost unerring goalkicking.

But he took some time to convince the All Blacks selectors of his merits. First picked for the 1985 tour of South Africa – which was later abandoned due to apartheid – he finally made his debut in Argentina in 1985.

He had to wait until the first game of the 1987 World Cup for his home debut and he barely looked back until his final game – in 1993 – after he'd

masterminded an historic win over the British and Irish Lions.

"He is an incredible bloke, such a perfectionist and so analytical. He explained the mechanics of goal-kicking and changed my approach to the whole business," explained Andrew Mehrtens, one of the All Blacks who tried to fill Fox's No 10 shirt.

Fox was only three years and 12 matches into his Test career – in 1988 – when he broke the old New Zealand points scoring record, held by SuperBoot Don Clarke. He only needed six matches to reach his century of points for New Zealand.

LEFT Grant Fox the goal-kicking phenomenon who excelled in the 1987 tournament

GAVIN HASTINGS

Country: *Scotland*
Position: *Full-back*
Test Caps: *61*
Test Points: *667*
World Cups (3): *1987, 1991 and 1995*

HOLLYWOOD ACTOR MEL GIBSON starred in the famous film about Scottish legend, William Wallace, called Braveheart.

BELOW Gavin Hastings in 1993

And although Wallace is still revered across the length and breadth of Scotland in rugby circles they had their very own Braveheart in the shape of Gavin Hastings.

Readers of Scotland's Daily Record newspaper voted him the second greatest Scot of all time – behind Wallace – to emphasis the position he had attained north of the border.

And even though Hastings' last game was a World Cup quarter-final defeat to New Zealand he was still carried – shoulder high – off the pitch by Scotland supporters.

He'd scored 15 points as the Scots lost 48-30, and afterwards New Zealand captain Sean Fitzpatrick led the tributes.

"Gavin Hastings is certainly the best full-back in the world at the moment," said Fitzpatrick. "We began our international careers in the same year and so I'm a contemporary of his. Gavin has been a fine player and a fine ambassador, not just for Scottish rugby, but also for the game of rugby as a whole.

"He's shown his class again in this World Cup and he can definitely hold his head high."

Politicians even joined in the clamour to verbally pat the big man on the back. Sir Hector Monro, the Scottish office minister with responsibility for sport added: "I would like to extend my personal thanks for the wonderful memories with which he has left us all and for the manner in which he has conducted himself in victory and defeat throughout his very distinguished career."

Hastings – who started his club rugby for Watsonians – finished his career with a record 667 points for Scotland and a record 61 caps, the cap mark later overtaken by brother, Scott.

And minutes after that last match he was as modest as ever, preferring to talk about the team and the supporters, rather than himself.

"The feeling is one of immense pride, captaining Scotland at the World Cup and leading them for the last three seasons. It has been magnificent. At times it has been very hard, but you can put away the bad times and savour the good times," Hastings said.

"I'd like to pay tribute to the Tartan Army. The support that we have received has been fantastic and they certainly make themselves heard, that's for sure.

"Coming out here to the World Cup was an ambition of mine and it has been a great experience that will live with me for a long, long time. But now is the time to move on to new things.

"So far as today is concerned, I want to say how proud I am of the way that the boys came back in those last 10 minutes, when I'm sure it must have looked to most people as if New Zealand would score 60."

His record of 227 points in World Cup finals (three tournaments between 1987 and 1995) still stands today.

And in Six Nations terms he went out on a big high. In 1995 he scored a try as Scotland beat France – in Paris – for the first time since 1969.

Hastings – who was instrumental in Scotland's 1990 Grand Slam – wasn't just taken to the hearts of Scottish rugby fans as he captained the 1993 Lions close to an historic triumph in New Zealand.

Lions historian Clem Thomas remembered a gregarious captain on the 1993 trip "There is no man more respected for his abilities both on and off the field than this delightful Scot, who is the epitome of the rugby man; brave, resolute, adventurous and one who loves a party," said Thomas.

After ending his Test career, just as rugby union turned professional, he dabbled with American football when he quit rugby, turning out for the Scottish Claymores.

ABOVE Gavin Hastings clashes with Philippe Saint Andre of France, 1995

MARTIN JOHNSON
Country: *England*
Position: *Second-Row*
Test Caps: *84*
Test Points: *10*
World Cups (3): *1995, 1999 and 2003*

IT IS SAID THAT YOU NEVER KNOW exactly what you have until it is gone. And this phrase was never more aptly used to describe the influence of Martin Johnson on both the England and Leicester teams.

Both sides, and the man himself, would have talked down Johnno's influence – once he was gone – but the bare facts remain that with Johnson at the helm England won the World Cup in 2003 and Leicester won back-to-back Heineken Cup titles in 2000 and 2001.

Without him England spent the three years following their World Cup triumph spiralling down the world rankings and Leicester struggled to even make the knockout stages of Europe's top competition.

Of course other players retired when Johnson left the international scene and a certain Jonny Wilkinson was blighted by injury. But Johnson was the heartbeat of both the England and Leicester

BELOW Martin Johnson of England lifts the Webb Ellis Cup aloft after England won their match against Australia, 2003

teams of the early 21st century.

On that incredible day in Sydney – when England won the World Cup – everyone remembers that Wilkinson kicked the winning drop goal but few remember it was Johnson who drove the ball up the middle for the final time so Wilkinson could be set and Matt Dawson could deliver the perfect pass; another example of a man engaging in a selfless act on behalf of the team.

Regarded by many as the greatest English rugby player of all time, the World Cup final was the last in a long line of great games played by the Leicester lock.

He made his England debut as an 11th hour replacement for Wade Dooley – in 1993 – and then promptly put in a great display as England beat France 16-15.

And apart from the Grand Slams in both 1995 and 2003, when Johnson was colossus, there were the two games – against New Zealand and Australia – in the months before the World Cup win that defined him and England as the world's number one.

Long before Johnson lifted the Webb Ellis Cup above his head – in Sydney – he was guaranteed his place in rugby folklore.

Already an England legend, in 2001 he became the first man to captain the British and Irish Lions on successive tours.

He skippered a winning side in 1997 and four years later came within a whisker of the same result, before the side lost the third Test, 29-23, and the series 2-1.

He may have been raised in the Midlands with a mother who took him long-distance running to build up his stamina, but some of his tough edges were knocked off in a short trip to New Zealand.

As a teenager Johnson decided to try his hand at New Zealand rugby, in Colin Meads' King Country, and he even made the New Zealand Under-21 side before returning to England for his incredible career.

The New Zealanders would have loved for him to have settled in their country and played for the All Blacks. Luckily for England he chose to return home.

Allied to his success with England and the Lions he had an unprecedented run with his only professional club, the Leicester Tigers.

Under his leadership Leicester won four consecutive English League titles and two Heineken Cups.

Already the holder of an MBE, he was made a CBE in the 2004 New Year honours list and finally bowed out as a player on 4 June 2005 captaining his own team – at Twickenham – against one captained by Jonah Lomu in a benefit match. More than 40,000 fans came to Twickenham to say goodbye to one of the greatest living Englishmen, proceeds going to cancer and children's charities.

ABOVE Martin Johnson drives ahead during the Rugby World Cup semi-final match between England and France

MICHAEL JONES

Country: *New Zealand*
Position: *Flanker*
Test Caps: *55*
Test Points: *56*
World Cups (2): *1987 and 1991*

ONE OF THE KEY REASONS WHY New Zealand romped through the 1987 World Cup, destroying everyone in their path was flanker, Michael Jones.

Although a devoted Samoan when he made his Test debut in 1987 Samoa weren't even part of the World Cup family, so – with him living in New Zealand - it was a natural progression for him to play for the All Blacks.

Latterly he has become a key figure in the welfare of Polynesians working and living in New Zealand, particularly with his work at Auckland University.

He was taken to the heart of the New Zealand public as they voted him the third greatest All Black, of all time, behind Colin Meads and Sean Fitzpatrick.

Rugby World Magazine named him the best openside in the history of the sport, picking him in their Team of the Millennium.

And Wellington's Evening Post newspaper described him as "rugby's greatest role model".

He did much to define the role of the openside flanker we see in rugby today. He had great ball skills, allied with a powerful physique and the uncanny ability to follow the ball around the field.

Former New Zealand coach John Hart who coached Jones at both Auckland and with the All Blacks called him "almost the perfect rugby player."

Nicknamed 'The Iceman' due to his cool attitude under fire, Jones saw his career interrupted by two serious knee

BELOW Michael Jones runs with the ball during the Bledisloe Cup game against Australia, 1991

injuries, which prevented him from adding to his 55 caps.

Following his exploits on the field Jones was persuaded to move into coaching, where he became the spiritual leader of the Samoan team, first as John Boe's number two and more recently as head coach.

"In the Pacific we eat, sleep and drink rugby. It is so entwined with their sense of who they are, and their sense of pride, and being Samoan, Tongan, or Fiji, or even, you know, Cook Island, Niuean, Tokelauan, because it's just such a big part of the culture now," Jones explains.

Jones's impact on the game was all the more remarkable considering the religious stand he made stating that he would never play rugby on a Sunday.

This ensured that he missed a number of key games, but such was his ability the All Blacks continued to select him when he was available.

But as a man of principle he refused to break a promise he once made. "I had to make my mind up on the subject when I was 16 or 17 and I'm so grateful to the coaches and players I was involved with who accepted it," said Jones in the New Zealand Herald.

"But I know there were times when I apologised to players [who had covered for me] and some coaches probably thought it was a bit strange at first.

"You don't put God in a box in deciding what you do and don't do on Sundays. I know that I would probably struggle to get a contract now. For a young player in the situation now it would be a case of talking to the right people and praying about it – go to the final word. In the end it is a very personal thing."

That pledge even restricts his duties as a coach and if Samoa are scheduled to play on a Sunday Jones takes a "step back" from active coaching on match day.

"When I stopped playing rugby, people soon forgot the player and one thing I'd like to be remembered for is the one person who put God before rugby," he says.

"I feel that people who would never have heard about God, have done so because of my stand, because it's brought attention to it. I've been able to show people that there obviously is a God who must exist or else someone wouldn't be prepared to do that."

Doing the extraordinary was Jones's mantra, whether on or off the pitch.

ABOVE Michael Jones in action during a 1991 World Cup match against the USA

NICK FARR-JONES

Country: *Australia*
Position: *Scrum-half*
Test Caps: *63*
Test Points: *37*
World Cups (2): *1987 and 1991*

AUSTRALIA COACH BOB DWYER IS a man rarely short of an opinion, rarely short of an analytical view on a player. So when he describes a player's influence as "immeasurable" it is wise to sit up and take notice.

Dwyer was forced into such a claim when asked to consider the career of scrum-half Nick Farr-Jones, the man who lifted the Webb Ellis Cup in 1991.

Dwyer handed Farr-Jones the Australia captaincy in 1988 – after the sacking of Andrew Slack – and once he had decided to hang up his boots in between the 1991 and 1995 World Cups, Dwyer said: "His contribution is immeasurable, almost impossible to put into words. All you can say is that he could not have done more."

What Farr-Jones did do was help mastermind a remarkable transformation in the fortunes of the Australian rugby team.

No-hopers in the 1970s, Farr-Jones was one-third of the Holy Trinity – with Michael Lynagh and David Campese – that spearheaded their reversal of fortunes to such an extent they lifted the World Cup twice, in 1991 and 1999.

The three stars first announced their presence in the rugby world in 1984 as Australia completed a Glam Slam tour of Britain and Ireland, then going on to dominate on the world stage. Farr-Jones made his Test debut on that tour, kicking off his international career with Mark Ella outside him.

A natural leader, Farr-Jones was the obvious choice to skipper the side after they had finished fourth at the first World Cup. From the moment he had the armband the campaign to go much further in 1991 started in earnest.

That campaign didn't go that smoothly until a 1990 victory in New Zealand made the team believe they could become the world's number one side.

He followed some legends into the Wallabies' number nine shirt (John Hipwell and Ken Catchpole) showing leadership qualities that set him apart in the history of Australian rugby.

A sniping runner and fearless defender, Farr-Jones developed a great pass off either hand.

Central to his abilities was the half-back partnership he formed with Lynagh. Together in 47 Tests the two men set a world record for a half-back partnership.

Farr-Jones tried to retire in 1992 only to be called back for one last crack at the Springboks a year later. The series was won, clinched with a 19-12 victory and Farr-Jones could depart in style.

"Before we ran on, it (Farr-Jones' retirement) was in the back of our minds," Australian captain and man-of-the-series Phil Kearns said.

"One of the brothers has gone. That is disappointing but we are glad we gave him a win. We did not want to let him down."

After he retired, Farr-Jones – who captained Australia a then record 36 times – stayed in public life, with a successful business career, and in 1999 became an elected councillor in Sydney.

A law graduate, born in Caringbah, New South Wales, Farr-Jones is a committed Christian.

JASON LEONARD

Country: *England*
Position: *Prop*
Test Caps: *114*
Test Points: *5*
World Cups (4): *1991, 1995, 1999 and 2003*

WHEN JASON LEONARD RAN OUT on to the pitch at Sydney's Telstra Stadium on 16 November 2003 few people in the crowd realised the exact significance of his appearance.

He was after all only sent on as a blood replacement for England tight-head Phil Vickery.

Nothing unusual about that and when Vickery was bandaged up he returned to the action, sending Leonard back to the bench.

But in replacing Vickery, even just for ten minutes, Leonard had chalked up his 112th cap for England, overtaking Philippe Sella's previous world record of 111 for one country.

Although Leonard only made a handful of those appearances off the bench it was, in many ways, fitting for the former carpenter from Barking. The appearance was understated and that suited the modest Leonard.

The rugby world soon woke up to the gravity of his appearance and although England went on to beat France and make it to their second World Cup final, England coach Clive Woodward made a special mention of the player afterwards.

"I hope what Jason has achieved won't be forgotten in the aftermath of this game," said Woodward.

Leonard's achievement is clearly all the greater because he played all his rugby in the front row, either on the loose or tighthead, where careers grow shorter and shorter.

Woodward added: "Jason has been an outstanding ambassador for the game on and off the pitch.

"All of his caps for England have been earned on merit and his contribution towards four Grand Slams and our World Cup win has been massive over the last 14 years.

"He will be sorely missed by his team-mates in the England squad, the coaches, management and of course the fans."

The supporters, as Woodward intimated, took 'Our Jase' to their hearts. A down to earth grafter, so many England fans could relate to Leonard and the efforts he had made to make it to the top.

He endeared himself to his many of legions of fans by devoting some pages in his autobiography to his "All-time drinking XV" from team-mates past and present. Only Leonard would have done that!

Leonard – who made his Test debut in Argentina in 1990 – wasn't even that lucky with injuries and one neck problem, developed in May 1992, saw him have to overcome damaged vertebrae. He underwent surgery to remove a piece of his hip bone and graft it to the top of his neck.

But four Grand Slams, four World Cup campaigns and three British and Irish Lions tours later he could walk away from the game with his head held high.

Leonard started his career at Barking, moving to Saracens and in 1990 his rugby journey took him to Harlequins, where he stayed until he retired in 2004.

Leonard was lucky enough to end his Harlequins career on a high, coming on as a late substitute as the Londoners won The Parker Pen Cup and soon after he made his final bow at Twickenham, for the Barbarians against England.

He captained England twice, the first time in 1996 against Argentina, a match he rounded off with his one and only Test try.

After taking a break from rugby, Leonard – who was awarded an MBE for his services to rugby – resisted the temptation to move into coaching and finally, in 2006, became a member of the RFU Council, the body that runs English rugby.

BELOW Jason Leonard displays a commemorative number 112 jersey after setting a new world record of 112 international apppearances during the Rugby World Cup semi-final between England and France

BRIAN LIMA

Country: *Samoa*
Position: *Wing / Centre*
Test Caps: *58 (up to 1.5.07)*
Test Points: *133*
World Cups (4): *1991, 1995, 1999 and 2003*

TO PLAY IN ONE WORLD CUP IS AN honour. To play in two or three puts you in an elite club, but in 2007 Brian Lima is on course to become the first man to play in five World Cups. Simply the stuff of legends!

In the 2003 World Cup he broke the record of any player for consecutive appearances in the finals, running out for his 15th successive World Cup match when Samoa faced England in the pool stages. He bettered the record with a final game against South Africa.

But at the next World Cup he's set to go one better and achieve a world record mark.

Originally a wing, Lima has moved into the centre as his career progressed after making his tournament debut in Western Samoa's 16-13 historic win over Wales in their first World Cup match in 1991.

Lima is the only player from that 1991 side still playing international rugby.

Gareth Rees became the first to play in four World Cups, joined at the 2003 event in this exclusive club by Lima, Jason Leonard, Al Charron, Fabien Galthié and Pedro Sporleder. The youngest player at the 1991 World Cup, Lima has developed a fearsome reputation for his tackling, earning himself the nickname of 'The Chiropractor'.

One of those legendary hits came in the last World Cup when South Africa fly-half Derick Hougaard felt the full force of a Lima tackle as he attempted to juggle a pass from Joost van der Westhuizen.

But before Hougaard could react Lima came hurtling at him with a tackle that will go down as one of the moments of the 2003 World Cup.

"I was winded a bit, and it all went dark for a while," Hougaard explained.

"I had to lie on the ground for a few minutes just to get my breath back.

"I am still here so that is a good sign but it was definitely the hardest tackle

ABOVE Brian Lima is tackled by Danie Rossouw during the Rugby World Cup Pool C match between South Africa and Samoa, 2003

I have ever taken."

Lima played provincial rugby for Auckland and for both Auckland Blues & Otago Highlanders in the Super 12, before moving to Bristol in the Guinness Premiership.

And at Bristol he found a big fan in head coach Richard Hill. "We are putting Brian into the centre to utilise him a bit more than we have been," said Hill. "He has been devastating when he has had the ball and he has made an impact with the ball in hand.

"Brian brought international experience to our backline and is a massive physical presence.

JONAH LOMU
Country: *New Zealand*
Position: *Wing*
Test Caps: *63*
Test Points: *185*
World Cups (2): *1995 and 1999*

THE GIANT ALL BLACKS WING LEFT an indelible mark on the Rugby World Cup playing in just two tournaments – 1995 and 1999 – but still establishing himself as the competition's leading try-scorer, with 15. When he arrived – with a bang – at his first World Cup little was known of this 6ft 4in, 18st 8lb player of Tongan heritage, but four tries in the semi-final – against England – put an end to his anonymity. Lomu was rugby's first global superstar, a player guaranteed to pull in the crowds wherever he went.

Against England he went around and over some of the best players in the rugby world and ensured his place in the history of the game.

His undoubted ability prompted England captain Will Carling to call Lomu "a freak" and it was the biggest compliment Carling could pay the big man after the most devastating performance in the history of the Rugby World Cup.

It wasn't as if Carling should have been surprised by Lomu's impact. On his World Cup debut – against Ireland – he scored two tries as New Zealand won 43-19.

Lomu and New Zealand couldn't repeat the trick in the final, losing 15-12 to South Africa, but no-one was left in any doubt over the identity of the man of the tournament.

Keith Quinn, one of New Zealand's most famous commentators summed up his global appeal.

"Jonah was the most sensational player at any time, from any country, from any part of rugby history," said Quinn.

"If you travel to any faraway country where other sports are their national game and say you are from New Zealand, the locals will say two things: they will say 'All Blacks' and after that

'Jonah Lomu'. They don't say anything else. Lomu is a household name."

He first announced himself on the world stage at the 1994 Hong Kong Sevens tournament and his love of Sevens led to him winning a gold medal at the 1998 Commonwealth Games.

Lomu – who started his rugby career as a flanker before moving into the backs – continued to haunt England and effectively knocked them out of the 1999 tournament as well, scoring a crucial try that ensured they couldn't win their pool.

The records just kept coming for Lomu, starting it all off on his first appearance in the famous black jersey against France in 1994. At 19 years and 45 days he became the youngest All Black of all time.

And his achievements are all the more amazing if you consider he powered through his career with a debilitating kidney disease.

"Towards the end of 2003 it was hard to get through training – and the darkest point was when a doctor told me there was a possibility I could end up in a wheelchair," Lomu explains, even though he made an impressive 63 appearances for New Zealand.

That illness, which affected Lomu throughout his whole career, led to him having a kidney transplant in 2004, missing the 2003 World Cup as he had been put on dialysis three times a week.

Incredibly Lomu came back from the transplant to play professional rugby in Wales for the Cardiff Blues in the 2005-06 season.

His dream of playing in the 2007 World Cup ended when he failed to get a Super 14 contract for the 2006-07 season, although his bravery in actually making it back on to the pitch, made him one of the most admired sporting figures of his generation.

BELOW Jonah Lomu in action during a World Cup match against Tonga in 1999

MICHAEL LYNAGH

Country: *Australia*
Position: *Outside-half*
Test Caps: *72*
Test Points: *911*
World Cups (2): *1991 and 1995*

A WORLD CUP WINNER IN 1991, Michael Lynagh did more than most to ensure the Wallabies made the final of the second Rugby World Cup. Gordon Hamilton looked to have put Ireland through in the quarter-final with a late try but with just seconds left Lynagh completed an incredible move to score and hand his side a 19-18 victory.

"It captivated people back home. I heard endless stories of people kicking their cats or booting the dog after Gordon Hamilton scored to put Ireland ahead with four minutes left," recalled Australia captain Nick Farr-Jones "I heard of some who even went to bed assuming the game was lost."

Farr-Jones was off the pitch and even suggested afterwards that had he been on the field the outcome could have been very different.

Australia were handed a penalty and instead of kicking it, Lynagh took a tap penalty and set off down the field,

David Campese going just short, before Lynagh dived over.

"I'd come off injured and, sitting in the stands, thinking we were done," Farr-Jones added.

"Michael Lynagh treated the situation very differently to how I would. I would have read the riot act but he asked the ref how long was left and then said he would kick long.

"That (decision to run it) took guts and the rest is history as he went on to score.

"For sure we were lucky. One minute we were down and out of the World Cup and the next we were somehow back in it and on our way to face New Zealand."

Lynagh made his Test debut in 1984, retiring after Australia were knocked out of the 1995 World Cup, at the quarter-final stage, by England. Capped 72 times. Lynagh ended his career as the world's leading points-scorer with 911, a record later bettered by Neil Jenkins. At the advent of professionalism Lynagh joined Saracens and helped them win the Tetley's Bitter Cup.

OPPOSITE Michael Lynagh of the Wallabies in action during the Rugby World Cup semi-final match between Australia and Ireland, 1991

FRANCOIS PIENAAR

Country: *South Africa*
Position: *Flanker*
Test Caps: *29*
Test Points: *15*
World Cups (2): *1991 and 1995*

WHEN SOUTH AFRICA WON THE 1995 World Cup the team managed to unite a country behind them. The symbol of that team and the man inextricably linked with the Springboks victory was captain Francois Pienaar.

BELOW Francois Pienaar tries to gather the ball during the semi-final against France in 1995

Born in Vereeniging in 1967, Pienaar became not only one of the most important sporting figures in the new South Africa but he also transcended sport in June 1995, when South Africa staged and won the World Cup.

Just three years after Nelson Mandela made his legendary Walk to Freedom and apartheid fell, the picture of President Mandela presenting the Webb Ellis Cup to Pienaar is one of sport's most endearing images.

And when Pienaar reflected on the victory, he knew the Springboks had won the cup not just for the 60,000 fans in Ellis Park but for the whole South African nation of 43 million people.

"I've said it many times that no Hollywood scriptwriter could have written a better script," Pienaar recalls at BBC online.

"It was just unbelievable on the streets of South Africa. For the first time all the people had come together and all races and religions were hugging each other. It was just wonderful.

"Nelson Mandela said 'thank you very much for what you've done for South Africa' but I said 'thank you for what you've done'. I almost felt like hugging him but it wasn't appropriate, I guess.

"Then I lifted the trophy which was unbelievable. I can't describe the feeling as I wouldn't do it justice. If I had the chance I would have stood there forever."

President Mandela summed up Pienaar's influence inside and outside rugby when he wrote the forward to his autobiography, Rainbow Warrior. "Amongst sports leaders, Francois Pienaar stands out. It was under his inspiring leadership that rugby, a sport previously associated with one sector of our population and with a particular brand of politics, became the pride of the entire country," said President Mandela. Due to the sporting boycott that surrounded apartheid South Africa missed the first two World Cups and even though they hosted the event in 1995, they came into the tournament seeded ninth.

Pienaar had come to national attention as part of the Transvaal side that won the Currie Cup in 1994; the same year Rugby World magazine voted him their International Player of the Year.

Pienaar was relieved of the Springboks captaincy a year after the World Cup victory, by new coach Andre Markgraaff.

But South Africa's loss – as Gary Teichmann replaced Pienaar – became

England's gain as he arrived at north London club Saracens.

Pienaar brought success to Saracens as they lifted the English (Tetley's Bitter) Cup, finishing twice in the league's top three.

"Initially we were going to stay only a year. Finally we stayed six. It was a fantastic time," said Pienaar.

After he retired, Saracens owner Nigel Wray made Pienaar the Saracens chief executive, a post he held until 2002 when he returned to live in South Africa.

"Francois was instrumental in the transformation from an essentially amateur park team into a model professional rugby club," said Wray

ABOVE Springboks captain Francois Pienaar receives the Webb Ellis Cup from South Africa president Nelson Mandela, after the 1995 final

GARETH REES

Country: *Canada*
Position: *Outside-half*
Test Caps: *55*
Test Points: *487*
World Cups (4): *1987, 1991, 1995 and 1999*

WHEN CANADA CAPTAIN GARETH Rees strode out onto the Beziers' Stade Mediterranee on 2 October 1999, when the Canucks played France, he became the first person to play in four Rugby World Cups, making his tournament debut – as a teenager – in 1987.

Widely regarded as the greatest Canadian player he represented his country 55 times and even though his final cap came in 1999 his total of 487 Test points is still a Canadian record.

He retired after the 1999 World Cup but not before registering a 100% record with the boot in that tournament, slotting all 19 kicks attempted. His last Test match was the 72-11 defeat of Namibia.

In his World Cup career Rees chalked up 120 points and is one of the legends of the tournament.

"I've played in four of them, it's been a huge part of my life," Rees said. "I sup-

RIGHT Gareth Rees clears under pressure

pose I was quite lucky, I was pretty young at the first one and went straight through to 1999.

"It was an awesome experience and pretty spectacular to see how the Rugby World Cup has developed and how the game was changing around the event, so a lot of positives and a few negatives."

"With the advent of the Rugby World Cup people don't realise how important it is to a region like North America where you don't have the day to day coverage of rugby, a World Cup is something the press and sponsors can get behind."

The highlight of Rees's World Cup trips was Canada's campaign in 1991, when they made the quarter-finals and showed they had the potential to move into the elite.

They lost to New Zealand and Rees said: "The 1991 quarter-final for us was just special to be there and take Canada to that place in the rugby world which is something you only dreamt of as kids growing up in Canada.

"To actually be in a quarter-final stage, albeit maybe a bit of a mismatch, against a very powerful All Blacks side was special. We got stuck in and didn't concede. To be on that stage in a Canadian jersey was pretty special."

He was one of Canada's rugby warriors, a player brought up in the amateur era and even when the game turned professional he still kept the spirit of rugby in his soul.

"My dad always taught me that sport isn't about the score or who scored what goal, basket or try when," said Rees in the Times Colonist.

"He taught me that sport is about people. Yes, you want to be a success in the league statistics and you want your team on top of the standings and all that. But he told me never to lose sight of the importance of sport in other ways. That's why I never have trouble in selling sport to kids because I know what you can get out of it. It can keep you out of trouble and broaden your horizons through travel, even if it's just to the Okanagan for a tournament. You can't put a price tag on that."

Rees's esprit de coeur took him to a number of clubs, playing for Oak Bay Castaways, Merignac, Newport, Wasps, Oxford University, Harlequins, Bedford, and he was also proud of his performances for the world famous Barbarians.

After his playing days were over Rees became the chief executive of Canadian Rugby, a post he only held for 15 months.

BELOW Gareth Rees (left) passes the ball, flanked by Canadian winger Winston Stanley (right) during the first-round match between Fiji and Canada, 1999

JONNY WILKINSON
Country: *England*
Position: *Outside-half*
Test Caps: *52*
Test Points: *817*
World Cups (2): *1999 and 2003*

THE ENGLISH NATION HELD THEIR breath at 11.22am (GMT) on Saturday, 22 November 2003, as Matt Dawson fired a pass back to Jonny Wilkinson in Sydney's Olympic Stadium, in the World Cup final between England and Australia. The scores were tied at 17-17 but the nation needn't have worried as Wilkinson swung his weaker right boot to land the drop goal, win the World Cup and instantly become the most famous rugby player on the planet. After playing a cameo role in 1999, Wilkinson became – in 2003 – the leading penalty taker in World Cup history, with 39 successful kicks. "He is a very special player, a very special person," said England captain Martin Johnson of Wilkinson, after the final. "There is a lot of pressure on him and he gets built up to a degree where people expect superhuman stuff from

BELOW Jonny Wilkinson celebrates after the final match between Australia and England, 2003

him and most of the stuff he does is verging on that. There's no one you'd rather want in that position than Wilko.

"To call him a kicker doesn't do him justice because the work he puts in on the field and in all aspects of his game is fantastic.

"He is a very special player, a very special person."

Following the World Cup win Wilkinson endured an injury run that may have finished most players, failing to pull an England shirt in the following three years, although he did play international rugby for the British and Irish Lions in 2005.

Those injuries also stopped him accepting former England coach Andy Robinson's invitation to captain the side on a full-time basis.

His notoriety though, after the World Cup win, made him the most famous rugby player in the world.

A wax work of him was placed in the famous Madame Tussauds, he was voted the BBC Sports Personality of the Year and IRB World Player of the Year in 2003, following this up by becoming the youngest ever rugby union player to receive a New Year's Honour with an MBE.

Educated at Lord Wandsworth

College he was marked out as an exceptional player from an early age, making his England debut as a teenager.

His first start for England came in Australia – in 1998 – when he endured a 76-0 defeat as England toured the southern hemisphere with a weakened side.

And after playing at the 1999 World Cup, when England lost in the quarter-finals, Wilkinson moved into a golden period, which ended in the World Cup victory.

He's only had one professional club, signing for Newcastle after being spotted playing in Farnham, Surrey by former coach Steve Bates and taken north. His early development was helped by the fact that Newcastle were also coached by former England fly-half Rob Andrew, who initially played in the side, alongside Wilkinson.

"The defining moments in Jonny's life have been England's 76-0 defeat in Brisbane in 1998, going out of the World Cup in 1999 and losing the Lions series in 2001," said Andrew.

"He brought them all to the Telstra Stadium, Sydney on 22 November and shed the lot."

Chapter 5

The 2007 Pools

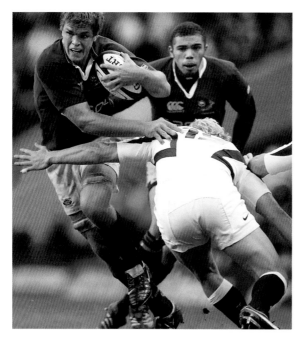

Pool A

England, South Africa, Samoa, USA, Repechage 2

THE ONLY CONSOLATION FOR England fans in 2007 is that their team's fortunes probably can't get any worse!

Since winning the World Cup in 2003 England hit the sort of form that would hardly have won them the European Nations Cup (Second Division of the Six Nations) not to mention the Webb Ellis Cup.

They fell from the world's number one in 2003 to the seventh-best side on the planet by the end of 2006 and bear in mind they had lost – in the previous two years – to the sides lying eighth and ninth in the rankings: Wales and Scotland.

So even though they are the holders they will certainly not go into the 2007 World Cup as one of the favourites.

They will arrive at the World Cup without coach Andy Robinson who departed his job two years after taking up the role in 2004.

Robinson presided over a shocking run of results in his two years in the job, culminating in them winning just one of their final nine games of 2006.

And to many the end of Robinson's reign, which came at the end of November 2006, was a release as much as anything. His position had simply become untenable.

"To some extent there will be relief in English rugby. It had become very messy and painful," said former England outside-half Stuart Barnes.

"They have not done it since he took charge of England. Their record as world champions is appalling – he had to go.

"From an English perspective fans will be delighted there has been a break from a failed regime. And that is what it is."

A place in the quarter-finals is the very least that England can expect and even if they show their 2006 form at the World Cup they are still likely to make it through the pool stages.

South Africa will naturally provide their biggest test at the 2007 World Cup pool stages but England know that wins over Samoa and USA – two teams who have never beaten them – will guarantee their passage into the last eight and a date with the winner of Wales and Australia's Pool B, in Marseilles.

England's recent history against South Africa is excellent although no-one would suggest they are in a position to repeat their performances of 2003.

When South Africa won at Twickenham in 2006 it was their first on English soil in seven attempts.

Andre Pretorius kicked South Africa to a deserved victory, after England threw away a winning position.

Conceding 13 points either side of half time, to go from 14-3 in the lead to 19-14 behind, was enough to sink an England team who were lacking in confidence after defeats earlier in the month to New Zealand and Argentina.

ABOVE Former England head coach Andy Robinson (bottom), feels the heat prior to his departure

OPPOSITE England will once again face South Africa during the pool stages of a Rugby World Cup

ABOVE Wallaby wing Clyde Rathborne is tackled by the legendary Samoa player Brian Lima

Losing to the All Blacks was expected – and accepted – considering the form of New Zealand – but it was the defeat to Argentina that struck at England's heart.

The positives for England in November 2006 were few and far between but it did signal the return of Josh Lewsey to something close to his World Cup form while a productive battle is building for the number nine shirt between Peter Richards and Shaun Perry, while Harry Ellis came back from injury in January.

Even though England's current form will be in total contrast to their form in 2003 one thing the two tournaments have in common is that England will have to overcome the same two key sides to make the quarter-finals.

Although the USA is also in Pool A it will be the games against South Africa and Samoa that will almost certainly decide their fate.

South Africa faced England in 2003 after losing to them at Twickenham a year earlier but this time the tables will be turned after the Springboks victory at Twickenham in 2006.

At the end of 2006 hooker Chiliboy Ralepelle was made captain when South Africa took on a World XV, becoming the first black player to captain the Springboks 15-man side.

"Winning the World Cup remains our main goal and focus," said Ralepelle. "There were so many positives to come out of the European tour in 2006. The young guys went out and did what the coach asked out in the middle, by keeping the structure. We achieved a hell of a lot on tour.

"The tour was all about getting everyone ready for test rugby. It was a great learning curve and we now have a good platform for the World Cup next year."

Coach Jake White agreed, adding: "The message is clear. Every position for the World Cup is up for grabs. I'll use the Super 14 performances as a benchmark for the World Cup."

White has forged a fruitful partnership with captain John Smit, who he appointed to the position before selecting his first team.

The Springboks weren't in vintage form in 2005 and 2006 but at least have the distinction of being the only side to inflict defeat on New Zealand in that time.

White won the Tri-Nations in his first year – 2004 – and with Australia's demise they finished runners-up in the two subsequent years.

At home they are formidable, completing a run of 13 successive wins in South Africa, ended in 2006 by France.

White won at Twickenham in 2006 after taking a calculated gamble of leaving some of his more experienced players at home.

Players like Jaco van der Westhuyzen and Fourie du Preez have the potential to be stars of the 2007 World Cup but most notably he has world-class players to come back into the pack.

Os du Randt is likely to play in his fourth World Cup while in Victor Matfield and Bakkies Botha South Africa may have - by September 2007 the best second row partnership in the rugby world.

This is only the Springboks' fourth World Cup after they were barred from the first two

BELOW Mahlatse 'Chiliboy' Ralepelle became the first black player to captain the South African team, a team England will have to face in their pool

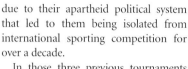

due to their apartheid political system that led to them being isolated from international sporting competition for over a decade.

In those three previous tournaments they have never failed to make the quarter-finals, winning it at the first attempt, when it was staged in South Africa, in 1995.

The World Cup win sparked a golden age for South African rugby as – under coach Nick Mallett – they completed a record-equalling Test run of 17 straight victories.

A number of coaches tried to repeat Mallett's magic but a semi-final exit in 1999 and one in the quarter-finals – to New Zealand – in 2003 were seen as massive under achievements in South Africa.

The 2003 campaign – under Rudolf Straeuli – was undoubtedly their worst. They came into the tournament blighted by record defeats at the hands of England and New Zealand, and they suffered the ignominy of last place in the 2003 Tri-Nations.

Straeuli was never going to survive a run like that and when allegations of brutality – against the players – at a pre-World Cup training camp surfaced, Straeuli departed, to be replaced by White.

Manu Samoa haven't had anything like the number of problems with their coaches in recent years and they are currently led by the peerless Michael Jones.

Jones, one of the greatest players to wear the All Blacks jersey, took over the coaching reins after the last World Cup, stepping up from his position as number two to John Boe.

The Samoans have already signalled their intentions to make this their most successful World Cup campaign by travelling to South Africa and Australia – in January 2007 – for a World Cup training camp.

The lack of matches between World Cups is Samoa's biggest problem, especially as the Tri-Nations and Super 14 tournament organisers have consistently refused to allow a side from the Pacific Islands to enter their competitions.

In 2003 Samoa showed their potential by rattling eventual champions

England in the pool stages.

The Samoans opened with a superb try from captain Semo Sititi and it took England until the 52nd minute to move into the lead.

The USA Eagles may be going places, but perhaps not quickly enough to make a big impact in 2007.

In 2006 they appointed a new high-level chairman in Kevin Roberts, the chief executive officer of Saatchi and Saatchi.

Roberts' first act was to recruit former England scrum-half and Gloucester coach, Nigel Melville as the chief executive officer and president of rugby operations for USA Rugby.

Melville in turn gave his backing to head coach Peter Thorburn, confirming he will take the side through the World Cup, even though they only qualified after a two-leg victory over Uruguay.

"I'm delighted that Peter will be staying on as head coach," Melville said. "Peter has really started to make a difference with this team and it's visible in the way they qualified for the Rugby World Cup against Uruguay.

"One of Peter's greatest qualities is identifying athletes with talent to play at the international level. He understands what the USA needs in France to com-

pete in one of the toughest pools at the 2007 Rugby World Cup."

Roberts set the Eagles the unrealistic target of making the quarter-finals of the World Cup Sevens by 2009 and the quarter-finals of the 2011 Rugby World Cup. One win in the 2007 World Cup would be an achievement. A place in the last eight, four years later, would be remarkable.

ABOVE USA's Paul Emerick breaks through Uruguay's last line of defence on his way to scoring his second try as the Eagles qualified for the World Cup

ABOVE Shane Williams breaks away to score against Canada in 2006

Pool B

Australia, Wales, Fiji, Canada, Japan

ONLY A FOOL WOULD CONFIDENTLY predict the outcome of Pool B in the sixth Rugby World Cup as it pits two of the most closely matched sides in the rugby world, Wales and Australia.

The Welsh haven't enjoyed much success against the Wallabies when they have travelled down under but you could hardly slip a blade of Millennium Stadium grass between them – in Cardiff – in recent years.

And because of the way the World Cup organisers have decided – wrongly – to award games to Wales and Scotland, as well as hosts France in this Rugby

World Cup it is in Cardiff where the Pool B decider, between Wales and Australia, will be held.

The two sides have met in the Welsh capital twice in recent years, once each in 2005 and 2006.

In 2005 Wales won 24-22 but in 2006 it was a rare draw, 29-29, James Hook tying the game up with a penalty in the 71st minute.

Hook is one of the new stars of a Welsh team, who failed in 2006, to rediscover their rampant form of 2005 when they won their first Six Nations Grand Slam since 1978.

Wales managed to lose two coaches in 2006, both Mike Ruddock and Scott Johnson departing the job, before Gareth Jenkins took over in June.

Jenkins' first job was to preside over a two-Test defeat in Argentina and the green shoots of recovery were not evident until their November internationals, when they followed up their draw with Australia by thumping the Pacific Islands side and Canada, but receiving a rugby lesson in the final game, against New Zealand.

Jenkins has certainly inherited a side with far more depth than the one that turned up in Australia in 2003.

In that tournament they were paired with New Zealand and after giving the All Blacks a fright in their pool game had to resort to wings over Tonga, Canada and Italy to claim a place in the last eight.

Under current New Zealand forwards coach Steve Hansen, Wales showed their potential in that quarter-final clash with England, losing 28-17 but leading the eventual winners 10-3 until just after half time.

In the backs Jenkins is as blessed as any

BELOW Matt Giteau could be a key man for Australia

OPPOSITE Chris Latham shows his ability in the autumn test between Scotland and Australia, 2006

BELOW Wales' James Hook converts against Australia

coach from the northern hemisphere and as his pack can win them enough ball the coach knows he has the match-winners to trouble any side at this World Cup.

In November Sonny Parker emerged from retirement to bolster the ranks and along with the established players he has others like Hook, scrum-half Mike Phillips and lightning-quick wing Chris

Czekaj to start piling the pressure on the established names.

Gareth Thomas will play in his fourth World Cup and in Martyn Williams, Jenkins has an openside flanker who can be the best in the world at his position.

Australia, World Cup winners in 1991 and 1999, and runners-up last time do, as always, have the back-line to win a World Cup but are struggling to solve their problems in the front five.

Those problems are so acute that new coach John Connolly tried a number of different combinations in 2006 and started 2007 with a World Cup squad that shocked many in the rugby world.

Gone was Al Baxter, who propped for Australia in the 2003 World Cup and hooker Tai McIsaac, brought into the team in the summer of 2006 to add bulk to a teetering front row.

In the backs Connolly has also lost two of the Wallabies' key rugby league converts. Wendell Sailor failed a drugs test – testing positive for cocaine – in April 2006, which rules him out for two years, while Mat Rogers has returned to play league.

But in Chris Latham, Stirling Mortlock, Stephen Larkham and Matt Giteau he has backs that are the envy of every other side in the world.

Australia have too often relied on the individual brilliance of players like these, rather than a team effort.

Connolly doesn't buy into the theory that the World Cup is all about who will finish second to New Zealand.

"We've got close to New Zealand in the last two games we've played, so there is confidence in this team that we are close enough," Connolly said.

"But we have to do everything right. You can make mistakes against some teams and get away with it but not against them."

Joining Wales and Australia in Pool B are their foes from 1999, Japan, who qualified for the World Cup with thumping victories over Hong Kong and Korea, confirming them once again as the superior side in Asia.

The Brave Blossoms will arrive at the World Cup with a new coach, after parting company with Jean-Pierre Elissalde and appointing John Kirwan to the role, just in time for the qualification process.

This World Cup will come with its own pressures for Kirwan, who won the World Cup with New Zealand in 1987. If they qualified for the quarter-finals it would be the biggest shock in

"He has a clear vision to win at least two games at the 2007 World Cup," said Japan's general manager Osamu Ota.

"He (Kirwan) has a long-term vision to improve the Japan national team, he has agreed to live in Japan, he understands Japanese culture and customs, and has previously coached an international team."

After the win over Korea, which booked their place in France, Kirwan said: "I am pleased with the team's performance and I am as pleased with the eight tries we scored as I am with having no tries scored against us.

"I thought we defended well and I must give credit to the team who worked very hard and wanted to play well. We can now set our sights on preparations for next year's Rugby World Cup in France."

the history of the World Cup but that doesn't mean an expectant Japanese public – with one eye on staging the 2015 event – won't expect victories over Fiji and Canada.

Fiji have been dangerous opponents since the World Cup started and in 2007 they have one player who could, potentially, be the star of the tournament: Rupeni Caucaunibuca.

The man they call Cau Cau has been the leading try-scorer in French rugby for the past two seasons and has the ability to turn any game.

Ensuring that Fiji and Japan will have to fight for every win will be the Canadians, quarter-finalists in 1995 and still a formidable outfit.

They lost to both Wales (61-26) and Italy (41-6) in November 2006 but that hasn't diminished the ambitions of the Canadian coach Ric Suggitt, as he left a number of experienced players at home for the European trip, instead deciding to blood a number of younger players.

"We were expecting a real tough game from Italy," said Suggitt. "They are one of the most improved teams in the world. They're big, they're skilled. Our guys, they played pretty well for the first half and then wear and tear caught up to us, and we were playing defence for far too many long stretches."

LEFT Gareth Jenkins looks on during Wales' training, 2006

BELOW Blues' (& Fiji's) Rupeni Caucaunibuca gets past the Crusaders' Aaron Mauger during a Super 12 rugby match in 2004

Pool C

New Zealand, Scotland, Italy, Romania, Repechage 1

IF THE 2007 RUGBY WORLD CUP were a horse race the New Zealand All Blacks would be 10 lengths clear, just coming over the last fence. Barring any last-minute mishaps everyone expects them to canter home to lift the Webb Ellis Cup for the second time in 20 years.

The All Blacks have of course been in a similar position before, most notably in 1995 and 1999 but this time they would need a stumble of Devon Loch proportions not to see the prized gold cup arrive back in Wellington in October.

Their main challenger is likely to be South Africa, simply because they were the only team to beat them in both 2005 and 2006 and New Zealand certainly won't fear any of the sides in their group at this Rugby World Cup.

The main difference between the 1995, 1999 sides and the Class of 2007 is their coach, Graham Henry, and of course the experience of seeing them fall at the final hurdle twice in recent memory.

Henry, along with his coaches Wayne Smith and Steve Hansen set about building not only a team of 15 to take on the world but also a squad of 30, and so powerful is that squad in 2007, the All Blacks second team could comfortably make the quarter-finals of this tournament.

They won all eight games on their European tours in 2005 and 2006, ending with a 45-10 win over Wales, leaving Wales coach Gareth Jenkins to extol their virtues.

"We didn't get any surprises from New Zealand. They are the best side in the world and proved that again here," explained Jenkins.

"Their ability to move the ball wide at pace was absolutely superb and was the difference between the two sides."

Wales' New Zealand-born centre Sonny Parker added: "The All Blacks are intimidating. From first phase they have a strong drift defence and cover every option. From second and third phase when you're trying to set targets they tackle aggressively and clean-out over the ball – physically they were stronger and more aggressive in that area and shut down a lot of our options."

New Zealand's weakness revolves around their inability to find suitable back-up players for their two key men, Richie McCaw and Dan Carter. Even when coach Henry tried to rotate his team both McCaw and Carter invariably found themselves in the side.

If either of these two players – or both – were to miss the World Cup the All

OPPOSITE All Blacks fly-half Dan Carter (R) tries to avoid a tackle from French prop Olivier Milloud

BELOW Lineout action between Scotland and Australia

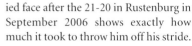

Blacks would be vulnerable but of course it is a big 'if' for the rest of the sides at the World Cup to ruminate over.

Targeting McCaw was how South Africa beat them in 2006 and his blood-

ied face after the 21-20 in Rustenburg in September 2006 shows exactly how much it took to throw him off his stride.

As writer Nick Cain put it in Rugby World Magazine, to beat New Zealand you have to be able "to floor McCaw".

If any side in Pool C gets within 10 points of the All Blacks they will consider it a moral victory although their toughest pool game is likely to come on 23 September when they play Scotland at Murrayfield.

Even though there has been an outcry over the ticket prices for the match it should still be a sell out and an intimidating atmosphere for the All Blacks.

The Scots ran into some unexpected form in 2006, beating both France and England in the Six Nations, before a victory over Italy gave them third place, under new coach Frank Hadden.

Those victories will give the Scots the belief that they can trouble the All Blacks on home soil, despite suffering a 41-15 defeat to Australia in the final game of their November 2006 series. That result was a big blow to the belief that the Scots could take their Six Nations form and turn it into a successful World Cup campaign.

Under Hadden the Scots have devel-

LEFT Romania's Petre Cristian is blocked by Spain's Javier Canosa during a World Cup 2007 qualifying match in Madrid, 2006

oped an impressive and expansive style that shocked the French in 2006.

Scotland's big test in the pool stages – if we presume they won't perform any miracles against the All Blacks – will come on 29 September in their final game when they take on Italy.

That game – in St Etienne – is likely to be a quarter-final play-off in all but name, the winner almost certainly progressing to face the winner of France, Ireland or Argentina's Pool D, all three sides vying for top spot.

"We are a lot tougher to beat than we used to be," said Hadden, and the results since he took over have borne that out.

Italy's only wins in the Six Nations, since they entered the Championship in 2000, have been against Scotland, so Marco Bortolami's side will be con-

appointment in 2005. The challenge is finding a true 80-minute performance from the Italians, rather than the 60-minute shows we have become accus-

vinced they can achieve second place in Pool C and their first World Cup quarter-final.

New Italy coach Pierre Berbizier has given his charges new direction since his

tomed to in recent years.

Although they didn't manage a victory in the 2006 Six Nations, they picked up their first away point in the 18-18 draw against Wales and only lost 13-10 to Scotland.

They followed this up in November by pushing both Australia and Argentina close and beating Canada.

Romania's ambitions will rest with the game against Italy and the final qualifier in 2007, as they present them with a chance of at least one victory, more than they achieved in 1999 or 2003.

A 48-6 defeat at Murrayfield in November 2006 for Romania probably puts a win against the Scots – especially as the World Cup clash is also in Scotland's capital city – out of their reach. And unfortunately for the Romanians the match against New Zealand is set to be nothing more than a damage limitation exercise.

In 2003 Romania were on the wrong end of a 90-8 hammering by Australia so all they can hope for is a similar scoreline when New Zealand come calling.

Romania qualified for the World Cup with wins over Georgia and Spain, the final victory coming in Madrid, 43-20.

They have based their strength on more and more of their players plying their trade in France and when they took on Spain, 10 of their side were either from teams in the Top 14 or Pro Division 2 in France.

Pool D

France, Ireland, Argentina, Namibia, Georgia

MOST RUGBY PUNDITS WOULD BE confident of picking the qualifiers – if

not the winners – from Pool A, B or C in this Rugby World Cup. But Pool D is on a knife's edge with any three of the major sides, France, Ireland and Argentina, capable of coming out on top.

France, despite their inconsistent form in 2006 will start as favourites. Their World Cup record is exemplary

and of course they have home advantage – and they have the backing of a passionate crowd – in every game.

But to the eternal frustration of every France rugby supporter no one knows which French team will turn up on any given day. The side that beat New Zealand in 1999 with a wonderful display or the side that disappeared four years later when they faced England in the semi-final, in Sydney?

Consistency, as England proved in 2003 and Australia in 1999, is the key to winning the World Cup, so France's biggest hurdle in 2007 is to overcome the dip in form that has haunted them before.

France had the misfortune of running into New Zealand twice at the end of 2006, being routed both times – once in Lyon and once in Paris – by the All Blacks.

But France's captain in those Tests against New Zealand, Fabien Pelous, is confident they can close the gap in time for the World Cup.

"I think the Tests are going to be beneficial to us as they showed us what we need to do from now on," said Pelous in L'Equipe.

"Contrary to what people said, compared to being swept aside 45-6 the year before, I did not have this feeling this time round. We were just murdered for losing some ball.

"The All Blacks are at an advanced stage, but they are only three or four players ahead of the rest – some of the back row, the wingers and (fly-half Daniel) Carter."

ABOVE Andrew Trimble helping Ireland on their way to a win against South Africa, 2006

illusions as to how close it will be in 2007.

The whole outlook for the Argentina team changed on 11 November 2006 when the Pumas won for the first time at Twickenham against England.

That victory will make the Pumas believe – rather than hope – they can pull off a surprise in 2007 and make their second quarter-final in eight years.

A place in the last eight could have massive ramifications for the Argentineans, more than for any other nation, as it would boost their case for inclusion in either the Six Nations or Tri-Nations.

Argentina's lack of participation in one of these major annual tournaments has been one of rugby's big failures in the last 10 years. More wins can only help their argument.

Argentina – who kick off the World Cup playing the first game, against France – have always had a pack to compete on the world stage but in recent years their back-line has emerged from the shadows

France's chances of making up the ground in time are increased as they have one of the most experienced coaches in the world in Bernard Laporte, who took over the job in 1999, moving from Stade Francais. Laporte's steady hand could be the difference between World Cup failure and success.

At the end of 2006 – and following those defeats to New Zealand – France did regain some of their composure with a win over World Cup opponents Argentina but as it was by a one-point margin (27-26) they will be under no to prove they too can do damage at the highest level.

Ireland went from World Cup hopefuls to genuine contenders in 2006.

They kicked the year off with a Triple Crown, followed by a promising southern hemisphere tour and then a clean sweep in the November internationals, beating South Africa, Australia and the Pacific Islands side.

While blowing Australia away in the first 40 minutes of that game they showed the sort of intensity we have come to associate with the current New Zealand side.

In fact Ireland were the only other side – apart from the All Blacks – to win all their games in November. The run moved Ireland to third place in the IRB World Rankings.

"We're delighted with the way the month went," said Ireland lock Paul O'Connell, who has the potential to emerge as one of the best forwards at the World Cup.

"Three wins from the autumn when you have played two of the biggest teams in the world is fabulous."

In Ireland's favour is skipper Brian O'Driscoll, a world star who should be hitting his peak for this World Cup.

grown over the last few years. The way we closed out the games against Australia and South Africa was excellent."

With the top three battling it out, Namibia and Georgia will stage their very own Minnows World Cup on 26 September in Lens and they will both know this is – realistically – their best chance of a first win at the World Cup finals.

The two sides have never met in a competitive match but Georgia's form at the 2003 World Cup and their subsequent qualification this time around will make them favourites.

The Georgians went into 2007 ranked 17th in the world, the Namibians six places lower in 23rd.

"We have a captain who relishes playing in those circumstances and leading a team in those circumstances and that's exactly what we need," O'Connell added.

"Our work rate and fitness has been

ABOVE Georgia – in white – charged through to their second World Cup finals, beating Portugal

Georgia made it to the World Cup with a two-leg victory over Portugal, an 11-11 draw in the second game ensuring they got home by 14 points.

Namibia had a tough time in 2003 losing to Australia 142-0 and Ireland 64-7 but under new captain Kees Lensing they look certain to be more competitive this time around.

Namibia qualified for the World Cup for the first time in 1999, taking the place of the Ivory Coast as Africa's second side, making it through after recording a 27-8 victory over Morocco.

The win followed Namibia's 25-7 first leg triumph over Morocco in Windhoek, securing a 52-15 aggregate victory.

"Our attention can now turn to Rugby World Cup preparations and ensuring that we go to France in good shape," said Lensing. "We have a well balanced side containing both youth and experience and I am proud of everyone involved."

RUGBY WORLD CUP 2007 MATCH SCHEDULE

M	DATE	TEAM 1	TEAM 2	POOL	VENUE
1	07/09/2007	France	Argentina	D	St Denis
2	08/09/2007	New Zealand	Italy	C	Marseille
3	08/09/2007	Australia	Japan	B	Lyon
4	08/09/2007	England	USA	A	Lens
5	09/09/2007	Wales	Canada	B	Nantes
6	09/09/2007	South Africa	Samoa	A	Paris
7	09/09/2007	Scotland	Repechage 1	C	St Etienne
8	09/09/2007	Ireland	Namibia	D	Bordeaux
9	11/09/2007	Argentina	Georgia	D	Lyon
10	12/09/2007	USA	Repechage 2	A	Montpellier
11	12/09/2007	Japan	Fiji	B	Toulouse
12	12/09/2007	Italy	Romania	C	Marseille
13	14/09/2007	England	South Africa	A	St Denis
14	15/09/2007	New Zealand	Repechage 1	C	Lyon
15	15/09/2007	Wales	Australia	B	Cardiff
16	15/09/2007	Ireland	Georgia	D	Bordeaux
17	16/09/2007	Fiji	Canada	B	Cardiff
18	16/09/2007	Samoa	Repechage 2	A	Montpellier
19	16/09/2007	France	Namibia	D	Toulouse
20	18/09/2007	Scotland	Romania	C	Edinburgh
21	19/09/2007	Italy	Repechage 1	C	Paris
22	20/09/2007	Wales	Japan	B	Cardiff
23	21/09/2007	France	Ireland	D	St Denis
24	22/09/2007	South Africa	Repechage 2	A	Lens

M	DATE	TEAM 1	TEAM 2	POOL	VENUE
25	22/09/2007	England	Samoa	A	Nantes
26	22/09/2007	Argentina	Namibia	D	Marseille
27	23/09/2007	Australia	Fiji	B	Montpellier
28	23/09/2007	Scotland	New Zealand	C	Edinburgh
29	25/09/2007	Canada	Japan	B	Bordeaux
30	25/09/2007	Romania	Repechage 1	C	Toulouse
31	26/09/2007	Georgia	Namibia	D	Lens
32	26/09/2007	Samoa	USA	A	St Etienne
33	28/09/2007	England	Repechage 2	A	Paris
34	29/09/2007	New Zealand	Romania	C	Toulouse
35	29/09/2007	Australia	Canada	B	Bordeaux
36	29/09/2007	Wales	Fiji	B	Nantes
37	29/09/2007	Scotland	Italy	C	St Etienne
38	30/09/2007	France	Georgia	D	Marseille
39	30/09/2007	Ireland	Argentina	D	Paris
40	30/09/2007	South Africa	USA	A	Montpellier
41	06/10/2007	W Pool B	RU Pool A	QF1	Marseille
42	06/10/2007	W Pool C	RU Pool D	QF2	Cardiff
43	07/10/2007	W Pool A	RU Pool B	QF3	Marseille
44	07/10/2007	W Pool D	RU Pool C	QF4	St Denis
45	13/10/2007	W QF1	W QF2	SF1	St Denis
46	14/10/2007	W QF3	W QF4	SF2	St Denis
47	19/10/2007			3rd/4th	Paris
48	20/10/2007			Final	St Denis

The pictures in this book were provided courtesy of the following:

GETTY IMAGES
101 Bayham Street, London NW1 0AG

Book design and artwork by Newleaf Design

Picture research: Ellie Charleston

Publishers Jules Gammond & Vanessa Gardner

Written by Paul Morgan